Perspectives on Culture and Society

Daniel Chester French
American (1850–1931)

Beneficence ca. 1928–29; cast by A. Kunst 1930; erected and dedicated 1937
bronze with limestone pedestal and columns

Ball State University, Muncie, Indiana
Erected in memory of the Ball brothers by the Muncie Community

THE PROVOST'S LECTURE SERIES 1987-88

Perspectives on Culture and Society

Ball State University
Muncie, Indiana

December 1988

© Ball State University 1989

ISBN 0-937994-12-X

Library of Congress Catalog Card Number: 88-63478

For information, address: Office of the Provost,
Ball State University, Muncie, Indiana 47306.
Printed in the United States of America.

89139 up

Contents

- vii   Foreword
  Warren Vander Hill

- xi   Acknowledgements
  Warren Vander Hill

- 1   Problems of Communication
  Daphne Park

- 15   Museums as Learning Centers
  Janet W. Solinger

- 31   What Information Revolution?
  Brian Winston

- 47   With the Mind's Eye . . .
  Karl J. Weintraub

- 63   National Service in America:
  An Idea Whose Time Is Coming
  Charles C. Moskos

- 81   Religion as a Community Resource
  Bryan R. Wilson

- 101   American Influences on
  the Development of Religion
  Bryan R. Wilson

119 The Premise of
    the U.S. Constitutional System
    Paul Sarbanes

127 The Art of Diplomacy
    Sir Peter Ramsbotham

149 The Continuity of Greek Culture
    Bernard M. W. Knox

165 Lecturers
    Provost's Lecture Series 1985–88

Foreword

Distinguished guest lecturers are a tradition at Ball State University. As I reflect upon my two decades at this institution, I remember with much pleasure the presentations of such persons as Sir Steven Runciman, historian and authority on Byzantine civilization; Dr. James Billington, the recently inaugurated librarian of Congress; Sir Ronald Syme, former Camden Professor of Ancient History and Fellow of Wolfson College, Oxford; and Lord Briggs, the provost of Worcester College, Oxford. A historian by profession, I have found especially stimulating the opportunity to hear speakers from other academic disciplines ranging from art to military science to theology. These lecturers have represented universities scattered from Cambridge to Colgate to Chicago to Berkeley. They have held appointments at the Smithsonian Institution, the Center for Hellenic Studies, Dumbarton Oaks, and the British Academy. Among them have been United States senators and representatives, State Department officials, and members of the House of Lords. Journalists, too, have appeared on the speaker's platform from the *London Observer*, the *Guardian*, the *New York Times,* and the *Washington Post.* As an attentive member of many lecture audiences at Ball State, I have witnessed a vast array of extraordinary scholarship and ability!

Many of these lectures came about because professors and administrators took the initiative to invite former teachers, colleagues, friends and students to our campus. Presentations have been delivered under the auspices of the Greek Studies Program, the Center for Middletown Studies, the

Office of the Provost, and the Sir Norman Angell and Stephen J., Sr., and Beatrice Brademas Lecture funds. I might add that these lecturers have often come at minimal cost to the university.

In 1985, as a result of the decision to formalize the arrangements that had been working so well, two events took place. First, a Distinguished Lecturers Committee was formed to assist President John Worthen in bringing to campus annually one or two speakers of very high profile. Since then, large audiences at Emens Auditorium have enjoyed President Gerald Ford, Dr. Henry Kissinger, and President Jimmy Carter—and there are more such people to come.

In the same year, Dr. James V. Koch, then provost and vice president for Academic Affairs, formally introduced to the university the Provost's Lecture Series. The first brochure announced fourteen lectures on the theme "Perspectives on Society: Past and Present." A budget was set up and administered in the Office of the Provost, and Professor John Koumoulides, who had already brought many fine lecturers to Ball State through his personal contacts, was named the official coordinator. To date, thirty-nine distinguished guests have appeared under the auspices of the Provost's Lecture Series. A complete listing of these lecturers appears in this volume.

A very natural development in the history of the series has been the desire to see the lectures in print. Increasingly, my office has received requests from members of both town and gown for copies of particular presentations. At an opportune moment, Mrs. Virginia Ball suggested, "Why don't we publish the Provost's Lectures?" And so it is because of her encouragement and financial support that we are able to present ten of the 1987–88 lectures in this volume.

However, these manuscripts do not represent the sum total of the series. I should like to acknowledge some friends and neighbors close to home who also graciously shared their experiences behind the provost's lectern:

> Dr. Richard Burkhardt, professor emeritus of History, former provost and vice president for Academic Affairs, and Mrs. Dorothy Burkhardt, former instructor of Foreign Languages, Ball State University—"Journey in Tibet"; Mrs. Virginia B. Ball, member of the board, Ball State University Foundation—"Ethiopia of the Past"; and the Honorable Phil Sharp (D-Indiana), member of the United States House of Representatives and former faculty member in the Ball State Department of Political Science—"The One Hundredth Congress."

Although their lectures do not appear in this volume, I can certainly attest that their presentations were most informative and well received. I want to acknowledge also the very fine presentation of Dr. John Demos, professor of history at Yale University, who stated that his lecture, "Ever 'A New-Found Land': Reflections on the Theme of Origins in American History," represented research in progress and therefore asked to defer publication at this time.

Now that I have reminisced about the origins and evolution of the Provost's Lecture Series, perhaps it is in order to raise a more fundamental question: *Why* a Provost's Lecture Series? Obviously, learned and thoughtful "outsiders" bring a larger world to us; they enhance our academic endeavor often in quiet and immeasurable ways. They bring new information to us, information that might not otherwise appear in the academic curriculum. Indeed, it is a special kind of information that is more than data, but rather knowledge that has both derived from and shaped their life experiences. This knowledge has enabled them to speak out in moral and ethical terms about culture and society.

For our students, these lectures often accomplish something that our professors in separated academic disciplines find difficult to do. Our distinguished guests fit the parts of an education into a whole. They also help students connect what they already know to what they need to know. And finally, they provide role models as people who have remained active learners while going about the business of living.

For those of us in the audience who are perhaps a bit older and more experienced, the benefits are not much different. Our guest lecturers become master teachers for us, too. They confirm what we have learned but perhaps not articulated and challenge our lazy assumptions; we are inspired by these creative, imaginative, and disciplined thinkers still filled with a sense of wonder and curiosity about what it is they do not yet know.

It is my sincere hope, then, that you, whether matriculated student or lifelong learner, will be caught again by a sense of wonder as you read and reread these lectures, ponder the statements that passed all too fleetingly before, and make their meaning part of your own life and thought.

Warren Vander Hill
Provost and Vice President for Academic Affairs
Ball State University

January 7, 1989

Acknowledgments

On behalf of Ball State University, I wish to thank the nine lecturers from the 1987–88 Provost's Lecture Series who released manuscripts of their presentations for inclusion in this volume. They have been most generous with not only their thoughts and ideas, but also their valuable time in revising these lectures for the printed page. As the manuscripts have arrived in my office, it has been my delight and privilege to peruse them and to recall the visits of such distinguished scholars to our campus.

However, publication of the 1987–88 lectures could not have been accomplished without the efforts also of Dr. John T. A. Koumoulides, professor of history at Ball State University. Dr. Koumoulides scheduled the lectures, spent many hours in communication with the lecturers, and collected their manuscripts for publication. I am greatly indebted to him for his continuing commitment to the Provost's Lecture Series.

I want to acknowledge also the fine work of Patricia Martin Gibby, director of University Publications, who personally edited the manuscripts and supervised the publication of them. In the multiple details of this endeavor, she was ably assisted by E. Jean Amman of my office.

I wish to express my gratitude to the many unsung personnel who regularly help with the Provost's Lecture Series. They include my secretary, DeEtta Rubendall, and the staff of Public Information Services, directed by Rae Morrow Goldsmith. The Office of the President also gives much valuable assistance in the hosting of our guest lecturers.

Ultimately, though, the credit for this publication must go to Mrs. Virginia Ball, who believed that these lectures were simply too good to be heard one time only and so made possible their publication. Mrs. Ball has been a wonderful friend to the university through the years and certainly one of the most faithful supporters of the Provost's Lecture Series. It is because of her generosity that many persons will now be able to read these lectures in print and reflect upon their ideas again and again.

Warren Vander Hill
Provost and Vice President for Academic Affairs
Ball State University

Problems of Communication

DAPHNE PARK, C.M.G., O.B.E.

Born in England, Daphne Park was educated at Rosa Bassett School and Somerville College, Oxford. In 1948 she joined the British foreign service and subsequently completed tours of duty in the Soviet Union, the Congo, Hanoi, and Ulan Bator. After retirement she returned to her alma mater, Somerville College, where she has been principal since 1980. She is also pro-vice chancellor at Oxford University, a governor of the British Broadcasting Corporation, chairman of the Legal Aid Advisory Committee to the Lord Chancellor, and a member of the British Library Board. Miss Park lists as her recreation "good talk, politics, and difficult places."

The following lecture was designated "The Twentieth Annual Sir Norman Angell Lecture" at Ball State University. Sir Norman received a Nobel Peace Prize in 1933 for his book *The Unseen Assassin*. In 1961, he gave his personal papers and library to Ball State, and in 1966 he came to the campus to receive an honorary Doctor of Laws degree.

I HOPE THAT YOU will not think that, as a governor of the BBC, I am about to seize this opportunity to address you on the transmission of programs. On the contrary, I am speaking much more as a former diplomat who served in three communist countries and two in Africa, where special tensions frequently prevailed. In those circumstances, and indeed in all circumstances, diplomats need to develop a capacity for the truthful reflection of what they see and hear in the countries where they are serving, and an equally truthful reflection of their own countries' views and policies. This is a nice problem of communication. It also, incidentally, requires a sense of history, since so many things in the world have happened before and will probably happen again.

One of the problems I encountered, particularly in our dealings with the communist countries, is that the same word has very different meanings for them and for us. Another problem is that journalists and the media, who are a powerful influence on our assessment of what is happening in far-off countries, have, except for the best of them, little sense of history and write and hear what they want to hear. Many of the youngest and most idealistic (and this is particularly true in Vietnam, where many of them served only briefly and had no previous experience of war) have a highly developed sense of national self-criticism—both a weakness and a strength of a democratic upbringing—and tend to apply double standards to a somewhat frightening degree.

As Natan Sharansky said in Oxford earlier this year, Elena Bonner, Andrei Sakharov's wife, had been astonished to hear an interview they had given to Agence France Press on the radio, as she said it sounded very different. All their criticism of President Reagan was there, and it sounded even stronger; all their criticism—and there was quite a lot of it—of Gorbachev's policy, especially his linking of SDI with all other aspects of disarmament, had disappeared. Who had censored it? Sharansky told her that he was sure no one had censored. It was just as in the good old days when they were working with Western correspondents: "They react to the things the world wants to hear. Today the world wants to hear that Gorbachev is good and Western leaders are not so good."

Take the process of negotiation. It is surely a basic need to know what each side means by that word. A Vietnamese member of the Politburo of the Lao Dong party, the North Vietnamese Communist Party, once told a Western visitor, "For us, negotiation does not mean horse trading." In fact, for any communist negotiation is a way of securing concessions but never making any. Le Duan, then one of the most powerful members of the North Vietnamese Politburo, said at the Twelfth Conference of the Party in December 1965:

> The problem of fighting and negotiation is not quite new in the history of our country. The Americans want to force us to come to the negotiating table for some concessions. As for us, our negotiations strategy must realistically serve our military and political aims.

The Vietnamese have long said, and have said it at many party conferences, that they negotiate to fight, i.e., to win time to fight, and they fight to negotiate. One element that never enters the discussion is the question of making any concessions. Indeed, they have frequently said that their position is "non-negotiable," yet they were able in the Paris negotiations in the 1970s to win concession after concession from the United States, which *did* approach the process of negotiation as something intended to produce a result through compromise and through give and take. For the Vietnamese indeed any readiness to give is a sign of weakness. At the Paris talks, the North Vietnamese secured the end of the bombing, the beginning of the U.S. withdrawal, the recognition of the National Liberation Front, and a splendid forum for propaganda; they made no concessions.

Freedom is another double-edged word, as is the word *democracy*, in communist terms. "Democratic centralism," for instance, means total control from the center. As Sharansky said to me, "In the Soviet Union the tap is turned off and on at the top." Article 38 of the Constitution of the Democratic Republic of Vietnam (DRV) states,

"The state forbids any person to use democratic freedoms to the detriment of the interests of the State and of the people."

Another well-known North Vietnamese leader, Truong Chinh, speaking on the 150th anniversary of Karl Marx's death in 1968 and addressing party cadres, reviewed the way in which the Lao Dong Party had applied Marxism/Leninism in North Vietnam. He said,

> In a democratic socialist regime, the enemies of the people and of socialism are deprived of all democratic liberties. The State and the dictatorship of the proletariat absolutely forbid them to profit from the slogan the "democratisation of the regime" to enfeeble or to destroy the dictation of the proletariat, or to refuse to recognise the revolutionary hegemony of the working class, and the communist party.

He added, in the same speech, that the dictatorship of a people's democracy must necessarily use violence against counter-revolutionaries and exploiters who refuse to be re-educated. This, he said, was why it was necessary constantly "to watch over and ensure the consolidation of the apparatus of repression at the disposal of a people's democracy—the army, the security forces, and the people's tribunals." This approach to democratic liberties enshrined in constitutions, but in practice denied to large sections of the population on the arbitrary decision of the party, is a not unfamiliar pattern that obtains in many communist countries.

What about truth? Perhaps the most forthright definition of communist *truth* was given by Ho Chi Minh, the admired leader of the North Vietnamese, who said in 1956, addressing the students in Hanoi University, after praising the ruthless Soviet suppression of the Hungarian uprising in that year, "Truth is what is beneficial to the fatherland and the people. What is detrimental to the interests of the fatherland and the people is not truth." Sadly, there is yet another truth that has come out of the harsh experience of the communist countries. Solzhenitsyn, in speaking of the experience of the camps, spoke of the bitter but absolute bedrock spiritual truth of a life stripped of everything but the essential, what he called the *lagernaya pravda*, that is, the truth of the camps.

Last, but not least perhaps, what of peace and neutrality? Yet another communist leader said,

> Our peace and neutrality policy differs from the double-faced neutralist policy of the bourgeoisie in certain nationalist countries. Our peace and neutrality policy is essentially revolutionary. The peace and neutrality *slogan* is a step in the struggle. It does not contradict our goal, which is to achieve the national democratic revolution, re-unify our country and build socialism in all Vietnam, but on the contrary represents an important and necessary step towards this goal.

Is is, I think, hard for us in the West to recognise how much of the life of the citizen of a communist country is made up in listening to propaganda that he, as a resident, wholly discounts but that probably fills at least two thirds of the official newspaper. In my own time in Moscow in the 1950s I well remember that the skilled Soviet watchers, following the procedures of the Soviet citizens themselves, found the most significant news in such items as the lists of Soviet officials and party men attending conferences and receptions. Absence or presence at a number of such functions in the Kremlin was a significant indicator of success or failure, and this was the real news.

Unfortunately, we have to allow for the fact that people brought up in this way find it extremely difficult to realise that, in general, we are free to express our personal views and are not bound by "the Line." Travelling on a Russian train in 1956, I met a Russian who spent three days questioning me about education in England.

Leaving the train when I did to buy food at a wayside station, he said to me,

> I know, of course, that you have to make propaganda for your country, and so you have to say these things, but please tell me the truth just about one thing—is it possible for a clever boy who is the son of a worker and not a capitalist to get any higher education in the West? I am a schoolmaster, that is why I beg you to tell me truthfully.

He found it quite impossible to believe that I could have been telling him the truth, and that I had been doing so without any special directive.

Two years ago, some of the undergraduates from my college were in Leningrad. Passing a bookshop with some Soviet students, they were asked by one of them, "Is it really true that in the West you can go into a bookshop and buy or order any book you wish?" When they said yes, he sighed and said that was his dream, to be free to read anything.

Little has changed in those years since I talked to that schoolmaster.

I should not wish you to think that my object in giving this lecture is to make anti-communist propaganda. Rather, my anxiety is that the two sides of our world—and we have to face the fact that we are two parts of a world—may not be able to communicate on vital issues simply because we do not understand the limitations under which the other half lives, and they do not understand the freedom, and indeed sometimes the license, under which we live—though, of course, there are notable exceptions when each can cheerfully manipulate the other! It is desperately important that we should understand the differences in our perceptions, because if we in the West are lazy and do not work hard to understand what the communist leaders are really saying, we may pay a heavy price. They, for their part, must often wonder how on earth we have managed to continue to believe the propaganda in the teeth of the evidence. Some of us, of course, are only too much like the three wise monkeys who hear, speak, and see no evil, and that necessarily adds to practical difficulties.

One of the most important weapons the communist countries can deploy against us is not nuclear at all. It is what is known as *desinformatsiya*—disinformation. In the Vietnam war it took the form of spreading a series of myths about what the North Vietnamese really represented and wanted. President Nixon once said, "North Vietnam could not beat America. Only America can do that." And he reminded his audience that if the United States was divided at home, it could not be strong at the conference table. This is just as true today, when the United States is negotiating for a free world with an adversary whose brilliant public relations campaign should not obscure the fact that communist states have a stronger sense of history than we do, and negotiate to win concessions, but not to make them.

What were the myths in the Vietnam war? Very briefly, the first one was that North Vietnam was not really a communist state. The North Vietnamese were simple nationalists who had temporarily taken on a communist look in order to secure what they needed from the Russians and the Chinese. When the war was over and the Americans went away and left them to get on with their lives, they would, of course, revert to simple nationalism.

The second myth was that there were major differences between the North and the South in that the provisional revolutionary government in the South, the political aspect of the Viet Cong, was not communist at all. It consisted of a broad range of opposition groups of which the communists formed only a part, and South Vietnam, left to itself, if the Americans would only go away, would continue as a mixed economy with plenty of healthy capitalist connections and outlets, living side by side peacefully with a "socialist" North.

The next myth was that reunification was a long way off. It could even be twenty years. It would certainly not follow immediately upon the end of the war, but would be relegated to a very distant future. In any case, it would be a matter for decision between the two quite different and independent regimes in North and South Vietnam which would arise when the United States withdrew. This line was frequently pushed by the North Vietnamese, by the PRG, and by their friends abroad. Arising from that, the form the government was to take in South Vietnam would now be a matter for discussion among the South Vietnamese only, though naturally the Provisional Revolutionary Government, the peace lovers, and the "Saigon men" would have to share the power among them. The implication was that the Buddhists and a number of other groups would be fully recognised and have plenty of power. The future South Vietnamese state would, of course, be neutral. By a curious coincidence, both an important PRG leader and the Soviet ambassador told me all this in more or less identical terms in October 1970, commenting on the then new Ten Points of the Provisional Revolutionary Government put out by Mme Nguyen Thi Binh.

The evidence for the refutation of all these myths was freely available in the published documents and published statements of the North Vietnamese leadership from the very beginning. In 1970—at the very time this myth of a separate non-communist party was being propagated, and Western journalists were being told by independent and "neutral" observers that the North Vietnamese had a great deal on their hands at home and simply had not time to face the problems that would arise from trying to re-unify the country, especially given the economic disparities—Pham van Dong, the prime minister, had publicly restated that the Lao Dong Party, that is, the North Vietnamese communist party, was simultaneously directing a socialist revolution in the North and a national democratic revolution in the South, and that they were indivisible. Truong Chinh, the party theoretician (the North Vietnamese equivalent of Suslov), had frequently outlined the tactics for forming a front and dominating it. He said in 1968,

> The party must keep in sight all the possible allies in a given revolution in order to assemble the revolutionary forces, acquire allies, rally to itself all those ready to be rallied, *neutralise* all those not willing to be rallied. There are alliances which will last through a strategic stage of the revolution, and temporary alliances, valid only for a given period in that stage of the revolution, alliances made to secure unity of action, and alliances made in order to neutralise. It is desirable to have a large united Front. It must be firmly directed by the Party, which cannot share this direction with any other Party whatever.

It was impossible to believe that the DRV had fought a long war and the socialist countries had given aid on a large scale with the object of allowing a non-communist regime to emerge in South Vietnam. Moreover, Truong Chinh, Le Duan, and General Giap had all frequently repeated that revolutionary violence was the only way to power in the South, and the "peaceful transition" was a revisionist error.

Finally, Truong Chinh had said in the same 1968 speech,

> The applications of our revolutionary tactic in the two zones of the country have been particularly fruitful. In the North the tactic serves the strategy of the socialist revolution; in the South, the strategy of the national democratic People's revolution. The different conditions obtaining in the two zones have determined two different tactics, and even two different revolutionary strategies. Without understanding this it is impossible to understand the spirit of the political programme of the National Liberation Front, or even to understand such a concrete question as the reason why the NLF has put out

the slogan, "All for the Front, all for victory," while in the North our slogan is, "All for victory over the U.S. aggressor."

Every Vietnamese understood the objective—immediate re-unification by force once the United States withdrew. But the world wanted to believe it when they were told that black was white.

There were a great many other sub-myths I will not trouble you with now, interesting though they were at the time. But what was the effect?

The effect was that America, and indeed the world in general, felt, as they were meant to feel, that they were fighting a bloody, unnecessary, and unjust war against a small poor people who only wanted to be left in peace and had no intention of forcing their own communist way of life (which in any case they had only temporarily assumed in order to secure the support of the Soviet Union and China) on the rest of the country. The rest of the country, i.e., South Vietnam, would freely pursue its own mixed-economy, capitalist path under a new, broadly based government embracing the religious groups and just possibly one or two leftwing groups. Laos and Cambodia would be left to pursue their own independent paths. In short, the Americans had created a communist bogey out of nothing and had dreamed up an absurd domino theory, and in the process, supported a tyrannical and corrupt regime in South Vietnam. There was, alas, some truth in the last statement, but there were also very large numbers of decent Vietnamese, to say nothing of the hill tribes, the MEOS, many of whom had voted with their feet in fleeing from the North earlier, and who needed to be protected. It seemed right and proper at the time, therefore, to let the Vietnamese settle their own destiny and to bring home young Americans who were precious to the nation and who could now live instead of dying. I happen to think that the United States became committed to Vietnam in the Kennedy years for honorable reasons, drawing on the lessons of Korea, and withdrew, so far as the American public was concerned, in good faith. But I also believe, without in any way denying the courage of the North Vietnamese troops, that it was the myths that won the war for the North Vietnamese. Hence, the importance of communications.

We need to understand the subliminal mysteries behind each encounter with these monolithic states. It is hard for us to remember the simple fact that, in communist countries—and I have to say that the same is effectively true of South Africa—the people cannot change their government by going to the polls as we can, and they cannot vote with their feet to leave because they cannot do so without an exit visa. When, as I quoted him earlier, Natan Sharansky said to me in Oxford only this year, "The tap is turned on and off at the top in the Soviet Union," he added, "There is no such thing as pressure for change from the people, because there is no machinery for this."

The man in the street whom you meet in Moscow or Tbilisi or in Kiev is absolutely sincere when he tells you that the people of the USSR want peace. So is the man in New York, or Alabama, or Chicago. The difference is that the second man can make choices. He can change his government, and he can freely choose between opposing ideas, freely and publicly presented to him. There is no monolithic single "line" of official thought in our countries.

I would not wish to suggest that there are not equal degrees of tyranny and dictatorship, equally closed societies outside the communist sphere of influence. If I have concentrated on the Soviet Union and North Vietnam, it is because, in their different ways, they have deeply affected, and can continue to affect, the lives of millions outside their own countries. For this reason we need to understand them and to convey to them, for instance, the fact that despite our instincts for concessions and compromise in the search for the preservation of peace, some things are non-negotiable, and there is a point beyond which we should not be moved. It is a matter for the judgment of our statesmen what that point is, but it does no harm for the principle to be recognised and understood by our adversaries.

Here I must add that I would not wish you to believe either that I reject the whole concept of *glasnost*, nor that I believe that our own Western world is perfect. But I cannot help remembering that, in Khrushchev's time, there was a brief flowering of limited freedom in the Soviet Union when thousands were released from the camps (and not, as Sharansky has pointed out, only 147), and a similar phenomenon apparently in China when Mao ordered that a thousand flowers should bloom. Certainly, in China, those who unwisely used their freedom to speak freely found that the heads of the flowers were cut off; and I think we must expect a certain degree of reserve and caution on the part of many in the Soviet Union precisely because *glasnost* can be withdrawn at any time, something that could not happen in a democratic country.

But we must also remember that many of our prized freedoms are genuinely difficult to understand for those who do not enjoy them. I had occasion to meet a large group of defectors from the North Vietnamese forces in Saigon in the 1970s when I was given leave by the Foreign Office to attempt a short review of North Vietnamese party policies. I had been talking to this group about party directives and party theory in both North Vietnam and the PRG. At the end of our series of conversations, they asked me why I had not sought from them their view of the West and the world they had now come to live in. When I put this question, they replied, almost unanimously, that they were made profoundly unhappy and uneasy by the fact that they no longer had a framework for their lives. They were told neither what to do nor what to think. They felt that this showed a lack of organization and left them in a deplorable limbo of having to think and act for themselves. This complaint was perfectly genuine, and I believe this freedom to make choices is truly difficult for those who do not live in our world to understand.

I said that I had also served in two African countries in which a certain amount of tension had prevailed, making successful communication extremely important. The first of these was the Congo, now Zaire, where I arrived to serve at our Consulate General in 1959. I left on posting at the end of 1961, returning, however, to the country from time to time since I had gone on to serve on an African desk in London and subsequently in Zambia, to the South.

In the Congo the lack of communication and the resulting misunderstandings chiefly arose between the United Nations forces and the Congolese. The United Nations forces were unable to understand that, although the Congo entered upon its independence with only twelve graduates, universal primary education but no secondary education, and not a single trained civil servant, doctor, lawyer, or professional of any kind (in marked contrast to, for instance, Nigeria), and although the Congolese leaders had no experience either of a Western economic infrastructure, nor indeed of the world outside the Congo, they were not primitive and certainly not children. Many of them had carried responsibility in a tribal structure and were mature, thoughtful men who needed to be taught how to operate in a wholly unfamiliar world. The first thing that they needed was to be given some respect: I believe inability to respect the human dignity of others usually leads to serious problems of communication. Much of the human waste and grief that resulted from the mutiny and the troubles that followed might have been avoided if there had been more mutual understanding and respect between the U.N. peacekeeping force and the people who so much needed a space to breathe.

In Vietnam, years of costly struggle against the communist regime of North Vietnam, in which many American and Vietnamese lives were lost or blighted, were wasted because the American public believed the myths and failed to believe in their own ethos. What greater failure of communication could there be?

Museums as Learning Centers
JANET W. SOLINGER

Janet Solinger earned a B.A. degree in English literature from the University of Cincinnati and an M.A. in arts administration from New York University. She was administrator of the Jewish Museum from 1961 to 1965 and director of Public Information and Special Events at N.Y.U. for the next seven years. Since 1972, she has been director of the Smithsonian Resident Associate Program, the cultural, membership, and continuing education arm of the Smithsonian Institution for metropolitan Washington. Overseeing a staff of fifty-one, Ms. Solinger directs a broad range of cultural and educational activities for young people and adults: a four-term course curriculum, monthly study tours, lectures, symposia, and classes in the studio and performing arts. The Resident Associate Program, presently serving more than 300,000 persons annually, is considered a model for membership and education endeavors of museums and universities nationally and internationally. In recognition of her many achievements, Ms. Solinger was selected Washingtonian of the Year in 1984 and has been awarded royal orders from Belgium, the Netherlands, and the Federal Republic of Germany.

DID YOU KNOW that more people visit the Metropolitan Museum of Art in New York in any one year than attend the New York Yankees' baseball games? That one hundred million persons went through the National Air and Space Museum in Washington in its first ten years, making it the most visited museum in the world; and the

Centre Pompidou is second, with 25,000 visitors a day? Museums are big business: they help to support their local hotels and restaurants, cabs and metro systems, parking lots, and street vendors.

It wasn't always this way. When the Huntingtons and Mellons, the Freers and Fricks, the Morgans and the Rockefellers (as well as the royalty and great patrons of Europe) amassed their huge and now priceless art collections, they were not thinking of the hordes that would view their treasures long after they were dead. They were grand acquisitors—buying railroads and coal mines, oil fields and banks. Buying art was another form of acquisition, another way of flaunting their great wealth. They were great competitors, both in purchases and in life-style. Preparing to build his mansion at 90th and Fifth, Andrew Carnegie, driving down Fifth Avenue, inquired of his assistant, "What does it cost Henry Frick to heat his mansion [at 71st and Fifth]?" The assistant didn't know, but Carnegie demanded he find out, because he wanted to pay double the amount. When they willed their collections and sometimes their homes, as J.P. Morgan, Henry Frick, and Duncan Phillips did, they were mostly thinking of their immortality. They would die and their empires could collapse or be run to the ground by their children or their grandchildren, but their art collections would be a public trust, carrying on their names and their tastes.

Until fairly recently, after WWII, the great museums were the province of the very few—scholars, the highly educated, the leisured class. Of course there were the school children who were led through the galleries, unprepared to enjoy the great objects and bored by the experience. Museums, however, were relatively unused, empty places, essentially catering to a small band of the elite.

After WWII, a series of phenomena affected museum-going. The GI Bill of Rights educated a whole generation who, in the course of their college training and exposure, became interested in cultural pursuits. New work regulations allowed for more leisure time. And the government, painfully aware of the support European governments were giving to their arts and heavily lobbied by arts interest groups, instituted first, in 1965, the National Endowment for the Arts and the National Endowment for the Humanities, state councils for the arts, and then, in 1976, the Institute for Museum Services. In the first fifteen years, these government agencies were funded increasingly higher and, until 1981, allocated larger and larger sums of money to museum exhibitions, thus enabling museums to mount ambitious shows that began to attract media publicity and new visitors. U.S. tax laws were written to allow corporations to underwrite museum shows tax-free, and at the same time to reap the benefit of the very helpful public relations the munificence brought them. Individuals, also through tax laws, were encouraged to donate art or to will it and to make gifts of money to their favorite museums whose clever directors, trustees, or curators cajoled and flattered them into becoming benefactors. By mid-1960, museums began to develop new audiences and constituencies. Perhaps the Met's purchase of "Aristotle Contemplating the Bust of Homer" at the largest price ever paid for a single work at the time, a purchase that was orchestrated with great media attention and dramatic presentation and brought long lines of eager people who wanted to be able to say they had seen it, was the catalyst. A *New Yorker* piece of the sixties sardonically noted that the height of culture was reached when the line at the Met reached the line at the Guggenheim.

At any rate, after the sixties, museums were no longer the quiet, contemplative, restful havens of the past. They began to vie with one another to show the most sensational art and to borrow and assemble the most extravagant loan exhibitions—to bring in the crowds. Will we ever forget the national tours of the treasures of King Tut, the treasures of the People's Republic of China, the Treasure Houses of Great Britain, the treasures of Dresden (treasures ad infinitum!), the Picasso madness at MOMA, the Manet madness at the Met, the great shows from the Hermitage, and so on? These shows of works mostly never before seen by Americans brought to museums people that had not ever thought about going before. People went to see, to be seen, to say they had seen, and to be *au courant* in the cultural scene. In the early sixties, on the night of his Leo Castelli Gallery opening, Robert Rauschenberg showed only plain white canvases, knowing that no one would look at the art, only at each other.

And the great museums—big enough to hold the shows, rich enough to pay the shipping, insurance, and installation costs of the loan shows, or prestigious enough to get big grants to pay for it all, close enough to large population centers to ensure attendance, and enticing enough to receive bequests and corporate gifts, individual large donations, and high category membership—became magnets not just for the well-to-do, leisured, well-educated visitors, but for almost everyone.

Government support has dropped since the advent of the Reagan administration with endowment funds stable or cut. The new tax laws that took effect in 1987 have had uncertain effects on corporate and individual support. But another phenomenon has emerged. Foreign governments are eager to have their culture—the heritage of their respective lands—seen by the American public. They are mostly interested in a Washington viewing, abetted by the director of the National Gallery of Art, J. Carter Brown, who pursues charmingly and relentlessly. (He will not take a show unless the gallery shows it first.) Recently coming exhibitions of Greek and Japanese treasures have been announced. Sweden is sending a major show to commemorate three hundred years of Swedish presence in the United

States. Canada is celebrating the opening of its new embassy on Pennsylvania Avenue this spring with a major exhibition at the National Gallery, and Indonesia is gathering its treasures of all periods and genres for 1991, when three Washington museums will hold major Indonesian shows. Just a few days ago a collaboration of the United States, Canada, and the Soviet Union was announced for an exhibition related to the Bering Straits region, shared by all three nations.

Most of the shows will travel. The last one mentioned will be seen in all three countries. Their main objective will be to help Americans to appreciate and to better understand foreign countries—once so distant, now increasingly part of the global village—Marshall McLuhan's once banal term—that we cannot ignore.

But there is more than the international exhibitions. The art impetus cannot be stopped. The Met's great Hudson River exhibition, the National Museum of American History's "Field to Factory" show, its latest exhibition on the WWII internment of Japanese Americans, the Museum of Modern Art's (MOMA) Frank Stella show—all testify to the power of American themes that are also drawing people. At MOMA during the Stella exhibition, crowds were lined up in front of the building waiting to enter.

The public is indeed responding enthusiastically. This year, for example, the Smithsonian Institution has been host to 24 million visitors in its first nine months; with three months to go, attendance will break all records. And this figure does not count the two new museums or any real blockbusters. Museums everywhere are filled, and visitors no longer go only to see the art. Museums have become meeting places, trysting spots, where the action is. In Washington, the National Gallery of Art's elegant, austere East Building, designed by I. M. Pei, is such a place. It has caught the fancy of everyone. Of course its great exhibitions—beginning with all the exhibitions I noted before and continuing with the big Matisse in Nice and now the Berthe Morisot show—have created great interest and high attendance. (Parenthetically, the much touted Helga paintings by Andrew Wyeth did not bring in the huge crowds expected this summer. We are awaiting Georgia O'Keeffe next month.) But big shows or not, its cathedral-height atrium is filled with people just enjoying the ambience and one another. They may never look at the art; they may just get a date for Saturday night. But many do look at the art. The young people in jeans, couples pushing baby carts, older couples hand-in-hand, students, visitors from foreign lands, visitors from Nebraska and Minnesota and Florida are flocking to the gallery, most of them eager to see whatever is on view, enthralled now by the modern sculpture, next by the exciting paintings, afraid they can't see everything by closing time.

And across the Mall, at the Smithsonian's National Air and Space Museum, thousands (the building can hold eight thousand persons at one time in the exhibition halls, and usually does) wait patiently to get into Sky Lab, awefully examine the Wright Brothers' plane and Lindy's Spirit of St. Louis, and exclaim over WWI and WWII aircraft ("I flew that one, son.") and the exotic spacecraft. The soon-to-be-installed Yeager-Rutan Voyager, which must be sliced in two to get it into the building, luckily arrives in early December, a relatively quiet time—otherwise the crowds would be impossible. The people are from all over America—young, old, punk, preppie, redneck, yuppie—certainly not the moguls of old.

And what else happens in that museum? The Samuel P. Langley Theater holds 486 people, and it is always packed for the newest or oldest IMAX film, from the all-time favorite "To Fly" to the now poignant "The Dream is Alive." The Spacearium—the museum's small planetarium—is always jammed with stargazers. And the shop is overcrowded; the cash register rings out sales of posters, telescopes, gyroscopes, slides, kites, toys, science kits, souvenirs, works of art, and vacuum-packed space food.

These two Washington museums are important examples of nationwide interest. In fact, museums all over the world have become much more than rooms of walls with objects and labels. There is a new kind of museum that was never envisioned when the great collectors of old planned their memorials. Let us now look at two of these new kinds of museums abroad.

The Georges Pompidou Centre in Paris, popularly called "Le Beaubourg" because of the district it sits in, is the people's cultural palace. It opened in 1976 to immediate world-wide attention. Even those who have hated the architecture—and many do (*The New York Times* critic, Harold Schoenberg, described it as "those silly smokestack—red, blue, yellow, green—ventilators in the plaza, the determination to be modern at all costs, the total conception, which is an alienating factor in the surroundings")—are forced to concede now that the place works. (Not always. I have had to walk up heel-destroying escalators into hot rooms without lighting during summer strikes more than once.) But it is an enormously important element of the intellectual and tourist life of Paris. The building stands almost as a self-consciously defiant exemplar of modern architecture and will eventually no doubt be accepted as a classic.

But it is much more than a museum building housing art. To go to the Beaubourg is to attend an endlessly fascinating show that is free and runs all day long, before you even enter the structure. In the large plaza surrounding the museum, young people from all over the world flock to perform and to see, hear, watch—it is their home away from home. They sit, squat, or lie down, listening and viewing for hours. And even the rest of us, perhaps not so young, can hardly tear ourselves away from the sights. We sit at ringside seats in the surrounding sidewalk cafes, spellbound. A magician is pulling scarves out of nowhere on the north side; a neo–Charlie Chaplin is performing in costume in the middle; a would-be self-immolator is coming ever closer to fire, and a sword swallower is swallowing. Sidewalk artists are painting away in staked-out positions. A violinist is fiddling a plaintive tune on the south side. A jazz trio, Chicago style, is competing with the complicated rhythms of steel drummers, while some country and western types, oblivious of their neighbor musicians, are whomping it up nearby. Unicyclists, mimes trying to evoke the magic of Marcel Marceau, and brightly colored jugglers complete the carnival-like ambience.

The museum remains open until 10 P.M.; a new sort of crowd arrives at 7 P.M.—the young professionals, the business people who stop on their way home or out to dinner. Now a jazz orchestra may appear in the plaza, and there is dancing or just appreciative listening. A piano somehow arrives; cocktail music fills the air. A lovely new scene is created. Inside the centre, theaters, dance performances, and films augment the art shows. The centre has five floors. The Museum of Modern Art occupies one, and there is a floor for special exhibitions. There is a public library, the recreated studio of Constantin Brancusi, a tape library where one can learn a foreign language; a movie theater that is a branch of the Paris Cinémathèque, the celebrated repository of old films; a museum of industrial design; and often special activities for young people.

The Beaubourg is making Parisians not so eager to leave town in the summer for their annual exodus—how can they tear themselves away from all of this fun and excitement? Through the efforts of the three different museum directors, the exhibitions continue to be first-rate; whether didactic ("What is Modern Sculpture?"), historical ("Paris/New York, Paris/Moscow, Paris/Berlin"), or fun (Claes Oldenberg's giant Swiss knife *cum* oars perpetually rowing away in the main hall). Clearly the Beaubourg, though somewhat out of the way (it is where Les Halles, the great Parisian outdoor market, used to be) and outrageously architected, has become the prototype of the new museum, with its marvelous outdoor activities, its appendages of movies, libraries, and film, along with the great art exhibitions.

In 1986 the small Picasso Museum opened in the Marais section of Paris, and in 1987 the much-heralded Musée d'Orsay, the site of a former grand railway station on the left bank, joined the Paris art scene. The Picasso is a lovely small museum situated in a charming former hotel and filled with the works of the great master and his friends. The d'Orsay is monumental, and contains French nineteenth-century art, from the academic to the most impressionistic, in no immediately discernible order. It is always crowded with people; everyone wants to see how a museum works in a train station. Both of these museums add to the richness of the Parisian art scene. And in front of the Louvre, I.M. Pei's glass pyramid is under construction, forever changing the face of the Tuileries, causing great debate and some consternation. We shall see. But we do know that the museums already in place have not achieved the holiday ambiance, the cachet that the Beaubourg exudes. They lack the striking location—a building surrounded by a dry moat—and the multifaceted purposes.

And now on to London. *The New York Times* recently asked whether New York City could support two *busy* Lincoln Centers. The question was rhetorical, the answer obviously no. But London does just that. The South Bank complex on the Thames opened in 1951 with three theaters: the National, Lyttleton, and the Cottesloe (the latter, alas, recently temporarily closed); all run by the National Theater, which moved there in 1976. The South Bank holds the Royal Festival Hall and the famed Hayward Gallery. This large art museum features the best of modern art from Matisse to Italy's fantastic new wave and the eccentric Gilbert and George. There are restaurants, bars, and an informal roller skating rink. The access is simple, a walk over the Waterloo Bridge, just beyond the Savoy Hotel. The complex offers promenading, good acoustics, and pleasant accessibility to its various locales. It works.

In 1982, Queen Elizabeth II officially opened the big and expensive ($300,000 million) Barbican Center for Arts and Conferences, and it has been going at full speed ever since. The Barbican's two theaters, the 1,166-seat Barbican Theater and the Pit, a theater-in-the-round seating 200, are both operated by the Royal Shakespeare Company. The London Symphony has its home there too. The Barbican was twenty-five years in the making. The name *Barbican* means the outer defense line of the city, and on sixteenth-century maps of London, the word can be found where the arts center is sited, not far from St. Paul's (although it is not so easy to find one's way from the cathedral). During World War II the section was leveled by enemy bombs; it remained deserted until the Corporation of the City of London decided to use the thirty-six acres for development. The $300 million was paid with City of London taxes, and the center is now subsidized by the Corporation of the City of London with an annual $13 million grant. It is surrounded by residential look-alike housing (five thousand people live there) and office buildings—called dismal by most critics. The architects have provided access paths, bridging a fountain-strewn lake, but this landscaping is marred by giant litter bins designed to look like rabbits, each bearing the "cute" slogan "Litter Bun."

The English critic Kenneth Robinson speaks for many when he says he is "irritated by the perversity of its layout." It is called hideous, out-of-the-way; locals liken it to Heathrow Airport and the set of "Clockwork Orange." Having found the center, you then cannot find restrooms or exits, and you find yourself in a vertigo-inducing maze of cul de sacs. It is meant to be an all-day promenading area for visitors, and it is not, because of the "millions of pounds worth of foyers, at different levels, underlit, and oppressive."

But nonetheless, Londoners have grown to love it, and even foreign visitors find it a must because of the fine theater, the interesting art exhibitions, and the brilliant concerts. It has become a highly popular amenity. In its fourteen levels, besides the two theaters, there are a 2,026-seat concert hall (the home of the London Symphony and pops concerts in the summer), a library, three small cinemas that can double as conference halls, two trade exhibition halls, the accredited Guild Hall School of Music (one hundred years old with fifteen hundred enrolled drama students) that has its own four-hundred-seat music hall and three-hundred-seat theater. It contains a lush greenhouse, elegant restaurants, bars, information booths (much needed), City University Business School, noontime concerts from Beethoven to jazz, and outdoor evening concerts on the roof in good weather for two thousand persons. People bring sandwiches and beer or champagne and arrive on foot, on bicycles, and in Rolls Royces. It is much more populist than its South Bank sister and strongly plays up trade exhibition areas and conference facilities. It is certainly not the hangout for the avant-garde that the Beaubourg is, but it seems to mean a good deal to the common folk of London. Its lake and fountains are pleasant for picnics and relaxation. It is now, like the Beaubourg, a major tourist attraction.

And where is the art? The Barbican 15,000 square-foot art gallery is larger than the Hayward, which has always seemed enormous to me. It continues to mount interesting exhibitions that people do go to see: "Aftermath," a three-month show of French post-war art organized in conjunction with the Beaubourg; "Aditi," the spectacular Festival of India show; a gorgeous and melodic Cecil

Beaton homage; and "The City's Pictures" from the City of London's collection are a selection of what has been on view in the past five years. This eclectic bag of exhibitions does not have any central theme: some are chosen from abroad and others are very local and very British. There have been attempts to put on performances in the art gallery in conjunction with the shows, but the spaces are open and directly above the library, so that noise is bothersome.

The Sculpture Court seems so far to have only two sculptures, described by critic Kenneth Robinson thus:

> Avoid Elizabeth Frink's sculpture of a moronic-looking streaking nude, and you should try not to be too nasty about the giant broken Rubik cube that looks as if it has fallen through the roof. Some kind widow gave this sculpture in memory of her husband, and I'm sure we shall never forget him, as we look up apprehensively every time we pass beneath it.

Presumably, the Sculpture Court will be added to, with the usual gifts, bequests, and purchases, and it is to be hoped that some fine Anthony Caros, Henry Moores, and Barbara Hepworths—Great Britain's three great modern sculptors—will soon embellish the Barbican. I must note that contiguous to the Barbican is perhaps one of the most interesting museums of all. The Museum of the City of London, with art objects, a diorama, and long labels, tells the story of London from its inception—the Great Fire of London diorama is a must for any visitor. Its direction casts a wide net with an admixture of art, drama, and film, higher education, and concerts.

The Centre Pompidou and the Barbican may be prototypes, but Europe is awash with new museums. In London itself, The Tate Gallery has just added the splendid new Clore Gallery, housing the glorious works of William Turner. London's National Gallery is adding a new wing by American architect Robert Venturi—what a blow to

British pride! The British Museum is always jammed. Brussels sports the world's first underground art museum—of modern art—built before Washington's. In Germany, new and great museums are opening each year in Munich, Cologne, Frankfurt. In Venice the ancient Palazzo Grassi has become a vibrant museum of modern art. And although Moscow has no new museums, its Chagall exhibition this summer—a first in the Soviet Union—created crowds seldom assembled except perhaps for the arrival of a very scarce food or clothing item. Every one of these centers is packing people in.

Back in the United States: This past year all over the United States new museums have opened their doors. The Terra Museum of American Art opened in Chicago. The addition to Los Angeles County Museum of Art and the Temporary Contemporary—which has been superseded by the wonderful Contemporary Museum—are in downtown Los Angeles, where no one used to go. The Menil in Houston, the new twentieth-century wing of the Met in New York, the National Museum of Women in the Arts in Washington—1987 was the year of museums. (I'll get to the Smithsonian later.) And both the Guggenheim and the Whitney Museum of American Art are fighting the zoning board process to add controversial new wings to their respective Frank Lloyd Wright and Marcel Proust classics. The Getty, again in Los Angeles, is constructing a new building (in Brentwood), and the Art Institute in Chicago has just spent a fortune renovating and reinstalling. Besides these, the Dallas Museum of Art has a new structure as of a year ago, the New Museum in Soho, New York, opened just a few years earlier, and the new Sackler Gallery of the Fogg Museum in Boston and the Building Museum in Washington both opened in 1986.

All of these are being built or renovated with the new, multifaceted public in mind. Now there are auditoriums and classrooms to learn in, gardens to stroll in, restaurants, shops—all the amenities that capture the non-scholar and that are making museums central to the lives of many people. Life-styles—they are a-changing.

But to get back to my story, a most salient example of the new museum concept is the Smithsonian's new quadrangle complex, opened in September 1987 in Washington. The construction all began with two proponents: the U.S. Congress and S. Dillon Ripley, secretary of the Smithsonian at the time. Congress wanted the National Museum of African Art, which the Smithsonian acquired in 1979, then a bunch of connecting row houses on Capitol Hill, to have a presence on the Mall, and Mr. Ripley wanted to have a Museum of Far Eastern and Near Eastern Art that could have loan shows—unlike our prestigious Freer Gallery, which carries a stipulation in the donor Charles Freer's will that it could neither a borrower nor a lender be. And then the third proponent appeared—the late Arthur M. Sackler, who gave his magnificent collection of Far Eastern and Near Eastern art to the Smithsonian over the Metropolitan Museum of Art's dead body, so to speak. (The Met had stored Mr. Sackler's collection free of charge for years.)

The results have been published nationwide, and I hope you've read about them. But not only are there these two fantastic underground museums set in the wonderful Victorian Enid A. Haupt Garden, where originally a parking lot and some unsightly, unsafe shacks used to be, including the one that housed Charles Langley's original experimental flying machine and that my program used for classrooms with much fear for the safety of our students. There is a marvelous underground concourse, three floors below—the S. Dillon Ripley Center—entered by a folly, a tiny kiosk with a gold dome on the Mall. Down there, in addition to offices, mine included, is a splendid education center with a jewel of an auditorium, state-of-the-art photography laboratory, classrooms, workshops, *and* an International Gallery. Day and night, the spaces are filled with conferences and classes, performances and craftspersons, children and families—perhaps six hundred at a time, enjoying, learning, creating. At night it resembles a giant university hall. The adults taking the 6 P.M. and 8 P.M. course sessions intermingle in the grand space presided over by a magnificent Richard Haas trompe-l'oeil mural as they arrive or leave their courses in art connoisseurship, the cutting edge of science, what makes cities livable, color photography, woodworking, music appreciation, and on and on. The Smithsonian is the place to be for singles, for retirees, for kids, and for families. All who partake find it fulfilling special interests.

I can hardly resist describing two relatively new programs. Every Tuesday morning (except mid-December to mid-March) senior citizens come to the Mall to enjoy complimentary breakfast and a stimulating lecture by a Smithsonian curator. Three to four hundred persons attend "Tuesday Mornings at the Smithsonian" every week, looking forward to this energizing time when they stretch their minds and make new friends. At the end of every series, the coordinator in charge receives a bouquet of roses from a grateful retiree. And the "Singles Evenings, Conversations, Champagne, and Canapés" have become an all-time favorite. Planned for working singles and registered by sex so that there is an equal number of men and women, this activity is emulated all over the world. First comes the lecture, and then, over champagne, music, and canapés, the singles may become duets.

From coast to coast, from country to country, museums are no longer what they used to be—no longer cloistered, quiet enclaves for the specially privileged. While still heavily engaged in scholarship, research, and conservation, they are reaching out to everyone, young and old, educated or not, of all ethnic backgrounds. Museum boards and directors today realize that museums need the support the whole community can give, and they are avidly seeking it. Mr. Morgan and Mr. Frick, Mr. Freer and Mr. Huntington would probably be aghast at all this activity taking place in the provinces planned for their friends and the scholars. But the rest of us are enriched by the opportunities that today's museums present to make museum going our way of life.

What Information Revolution?
BRIAN WINSTON

Born in Evesham, Worcestershire, the United Kingdom, Brian Norman Winston attended Kilburn Grammar School, London, and Merton College, Oxford, where he received both B.A. and M.A. degrees. Beginning his professional career as a researcher for *World in Action*, Granada Television, he moved rapidly into producing and directing programs for both Granada and the BBC. His work resulted in programs for *24 Hours*, *Talkback*, *On Site*, and *Newsday*. In the world of film and television, he has also been a consultant, an on-camera moderator, a host, and a scriptwriter. His scripts for WNET's *Heritage: Civilization and the Jews* received the Christopher Award and an Emmy for Outstanding Individual Achievement.

Mr. Winston is the well-known author of many articles and several books on communication including *Bad News: The Structure of Television News* (1976), *Misunderstanding Media* (1986), and *Working with Video* (1986). Now a permanent U.S. resident, he serves as dean of the School of Communications, the Pennsylvania State University. He continues another active career, however, as a guest lecturer and a contributor to such publications as *Punch*, the *Guardian*, the *Glasgow Herald*, *Sight and Sound*, and *Stills*.

"COMMUNICATIONS for the Next Hundred Years." There is a certain irony about this advertising slogan. It identifies a major player in the recently created, more competitive telecommunications world; but whether such companies truly herald the future or rather mark an inefficient dead end remains an open question.

Telecommunications over the last hundred years has essentially depended on electromagnetic carrier waves. These are modulated in various ways and transmitted either through wires or through the atmosphere. Bell envisaged the wired part of the system in the summer of 1877. He saw the telephone lines being just like gas or water pipes; and that is the model with which society still lives. The atmospheric part of the system dates, at the latest, from 1879, when Hughes demonstrated the radiation of electromagnetic waves. Within two decades the transmission of signals through the air point-to-point, from a ship to a shore station for instance, was a well-established technique. Broadcasting, first in the form of naval distress signals, followed within another ten years.

Whether or not such a communications infrastructure represents the best we can do for the next century must now be in doubt. For what should replace the vision of Bell and Hughes? At its most basic, this question turns on another more technical question—what carriers will be used? Only now has technology, in the form of laser-generated carrier waves and fiber optic transmission systems, produced new possibilities at this fundamental level.

So here is the problem: facing the move to laser carrier waves could, and I would argue should, involve much more than a shift to a different sort of signal. More is at stake than simply pulling up the old wires and laying new fibers. The possibilities raised by laser/fiber optic technology require that a fresh balance be struck between wired point-to-point and broadcast transmissions. Not an area of the telecommunications world should remain untouched, if we are fully to take advantage of this impending change.

For instance, we can now re-evaluate the correct transmission standards for data, video, and voice. Do we want to live forever with telephones that rely as much on the brain's capacity to interpret sound as they do on actual audio information transmitted? Do we want the resolution of the TV image always to be limited by the ambition of pioneers in the late 1920s to transmit pictures which were as sharp as amateur (i.e., 16mm) film then was? (This is in fact the basis of our current 525/625-line world TV standards.)

The full implementation of new basic technology could mean even more than enhanced standards. We have a chance to escape from the vision of Bell. We can conceive of more flexible communication systems which go well beyond the trunk-and-branch wires or the old transmission masts. We could decide to have telephones and computers which broadcast, or TV stations and newspapers which narrowcast, that is, which send different messages to each separate receiver.

Our confrontation with a momentous choice of this technological type is, however, not without precedent. It would be wrong to assume that this is a fresh moment in the history of these technologies. The system, although a relic of the late nineteenth century, has survived a number of challenges as severe as the one it now faces. That is why it has lasted so long and served us so well.

Beginning with telegraphy, the telecommunications infrastructure has accommodated the impact of telephony, of radio, of sound film, of international cables, of television, of satellites. There is however one major difference between those previous successful adaptations and our current situation. Almost all historical telecommunications developments took place in a regulated—normally a highly regulated—environment.

Currently the watchword is "deregulation." For the first time the system faces a major technological challenge not only without any centrally developed policies in place but also with the agencies that would normally make policy actively disavowing any such function.

Instead the hidden hand of the market will, it is claimed, operate to determine which of the options available are the fittest to prosper. Unfortunately, in view of past history and current events, the prognosis for letting the marketplace decide in the telecommunications field cannot be good.

Take the domestic use of television receive-only (TVRO) satellite dishes. A million and a half American homes acquired dishes at a cost of at least $300 million dollars. Without regulation these homes had access to materials not intended for public consumption, materials which undercut local broadcasters, and materials for which other consumers paid handsomely.

Signals were scrambled, and the providers of such materials as premium cable services discovered ways of marketing unscramblers and thus acquiring the TVRO owners as a new market for their product. Proponents of the free market might look at the outcome as being a fine example of the hidden hand at work.

I would take a different view. Deregulation notwithstanding, it took legislation (in the 1984 Communications Act) to make unauthorized unscrambling a crime. The marketplace in dishes pushed a technology which was, given the full range of technical options, enormous and over costly. The receivers sold to the public in such numbers were, after all, designed for industrial and not domestic use. The public's investment in facilities which turn out to be much more expensive to operate than anticipated can be dismissed by free marketeers on a "caveat emptor" basis. But there can be no question that the exploitation of TVRO has fizzled as a result of the increased cost involved in unscrambling signals. Sales fell 60 percent in 1986, the first year of scrambling.

The TVRO public in question is largely the comparatively signal-poor rural population which had been traditionally underserved by the broadcast industry. That TVRO owners should be relieved of one-third of a billion dollars and still have less access to signals than people in urban America is, at best, inequitable.

Moreover, this misapplication of industrial TVROs has stifled if not destroyed the development of Direct Broadcast Satellites (DBS). A much more affordable (because smaller) technology, DBS might have been encouraged, in a more structure-regulatory environment, on the grounds that it was the best way of redressing inequalities of signal provision between urban and rural America. A universal service rationale could have been easily proposed.

Further, a full-scale DBS operation, secure on its rural and ex-urban base, could then have offered a real market alternative to other terrestrial distribution systems (broadcast TV, cable, and various microwave applications), if such competition were truly desired and really desirable. For the moment, if not forever, the exploitation of DBS is dead, and the application of TVROs, even if sales recover, is stunted. A whole technology has been forced to wither by the marketplace.

The current situation of Digital Audio Tape (DAT) affords another example of the hidden hand's limited space for maneuvers in a high tech area. DAT is based on PCM (pulse code modulation) digital signal-sampling techniques first developed by French telephone engineers in the 1930s. Unlike its analog predecessors, a digital audio recorder offers perfect reproduction without distortions or background noise. A prototype PCM machine was demonstrated by NHK (Nippon Hose Kyokai—Japanese Broadcasting Corporation) in 1967. The earliest professional DAT studio recorder was announced in the technical literature in 1973.

Industrial versions of DAT recorders have, subject to the usual laws of the marketplace, been slowly replacing analog machines for the last decade and more in the recording studios of the world. The problem, as with TVRO, arises when the technology is offered to the public.

The record industry has been decimated by the easy availability of analog home recording devices. The Recording Industry Association of America estimates that the home copying of conventional disks onto audio cassettes is costing the industry lost sales worth more than $1.5 billion a year in the United States alone. In Britain, conventional disk sales peaked in 1978. In the half decade that followed sales of singles dropped 13 percent and albums 27 percent, whereas sales of blank audio cassettes rose 75 percent. To ensure growth and health the industry needed a new product, a new standard, whose essential characteristic would be that it could not be so easily duplicated. It found it in the laser disc.

Laser disks were first demonstrated by Philips as a storage medium for computer data. Since the technology was not widely used for this purpose by 1972, the company had turned the disk into a prototype video recording system. However, in consumer durable form, these devices made no headway against videocassette recorders: the superior performance of the disks was not deemed by the marketplace to be sufficient compensation for the loss of the recording capacity of the VCR.

The disks were then used to record sound and marketed as CDs (compact disks). A format was agreed upon between Philips and Sony that, it might be noted, immediately sacrificed one of the technology's biggest potential advantages—the capacity to record music at greater length than can either conventional disk or audio cassette. For an industry seeking to recover lost ground, this was not necessarily a commercial advantage. That there be no domestic duplication capability, however, was. If a CD disk is copied onto an analog audio tape most of its acoustic advantage is lost.

Since World War II, the recorded music industry has been particularly vulnerable to the technological storms for the sole reason that it lacks integrated hardware and software manufacturing entities. With the exception of Philips and now Sony (because of its recent acquisition of CBS Records), the hardware manufacturers do not produce the recorded software. Hardware manufacturers, largely in the East, have a vested interest in making it as easy as possible for the public to duplicate that software. The software manufacturers, largely in the West, have totally failed to stop them from doing so.

In October of 1982, the first CDs players were marketed. It is at this moment that the hidden hand becomes a hidden conspiracy to control the introduction of consumer DAT.

In June of 1983 no fewer than eighty-four of the world's electronic manufacturers formed the DAT Conference. This was done to establish standards for DAT as to tape size and PCM sampling frequencies. The manufacturers wanted to avoid what was seen as the previous decade's costly video standards war, which had pitched VHS against Beta. Despite the measure of agreement achieved, the problem remained. DAT would restore to the public exactly the ability to copy, indeed to clone, CDs. The CD advantage would be lost.

In this light, popular commentary which sees the non-appearance of DAT as 1987's greatest consumer electronic mystery seems almost charmingly naive. (And the notion that Sony's acquisition of CBS Records would facilitate its appearance is positively illogical, since Sony, by this takeover, acquired a vested interest in CDs as software.)

In fact, a technological stand-off has developed. Using the threat of European tariff barriers, Philips was able to protect its CD investment by having the introduction of consumer DAT delayed. It is significant that schemes to break the deadlock involve various nakedly regulatory solutions, from an outright legislative ban on the device to the required inclusion of circuitry within the publicly available recorders that would make them unable to copy CDs.

Already the DAT Conference has responded to the CD problem by establishing sampling standards for DAT which are different from the sampling standards used on CDs. This difference would prevent straightforward copying. However, the technology is not likely to be contained in this way. Even if the major players stick to agreements along these lines, fringe entrepreneurs can be relied upon to overcome any electronic barrier. The public could expect in short order black box add-on devices which will allow them the full advantage of DAT, which is the ability to clone CDs.

Again, proponents of the market might see this delayed introduction of a new technology as nothing more than the hidden hand going about its work. But is it not a curious and distorting free marketplace where eighty-four competitors meet to swap notes and one of them is able to use tariff as a threat to control all the others?

If DAT represents a comparatively insignificant problem in technological diffusion, the current proposal for a new world TV standard of more than one thousand lines is clearly of major importance. But a similar pattern of delay and distortion can be seen.

Twelve hundred lines would produce a high definition (HDTV) picture of the same resolution as 35mm film. A system using wide screen and 1,125 lines has been developed by NHK and has been actively debated by the world's broadcasting organizations for the last five years and more. Going to HDTV would not only involve new production plant and receivers, but would also require the use of increased bandwidths in the electromagnetic spectrum. The responses thus far have been typically hostile, and moves towards HDTV's eventual adoption are glacial in pace.

NHK was working with the American color system (NTSC) and American electrical standards (sixty cycles per second). The majority of the Europeans (who use German PAL color and fifty-cycle electricity) were immediately concerned with the "compatibility" of the Japanese HDTV. "Compatibility" means, in this context, the ability of the new system's signals to be processed, transmitted, and received on the old systems. In practice, the adoption of compatible systems would mean that the new system could be safely ignored by any not wishing to scrap existing studios, masts, and TV sets. The Japanese obliged the Europeans by demonstrating conversion equipment that downgraded 1,125 lines widescreen NTSC to 625 lines squarer-screened PAL.

The American industry, having closed its last professional television equipment plant (RCA), appeared at first to be solidly behind NHK's HDTV. But the pause enforced by the Europeans has caused a degree of rethinking here too. Now all the Europeans and Americans who had also been researching signal upgrades have started to unveil numerous less radical alternatives to HDTV. These would involve leaving the transmission system essentially in place but improving the picture quality by various enhancements. Since forty or more years have passed since the current system was determined, there is clearly a technological opportunity here. GE/RCA, for instance, has recently demonstrated an enhanced Advanced Compatible TV (ACTV) system which produces 1,050 lines and a wider picture but uses the traditional six-MHz channel.

There is, of course, simply no chance that the marketplace can be left to decide this issue. The FCC is necessarily investigating HD/ACTV possibilities. Any increase in the spectrum allocation of a single group of users, which is what HDTV would require, needs to be adjudicated. (Indeed it was spectrum use and necessary spectrum allocation that got the government into the radio business in the first place.) ACTV would move American broadcasters extensively into the UHF band, a move vigorously resisted in the 1940s. Others, however, most notably the land-mobile radio users, now have their eyes on this resource.

While the FCC determines this issue, the Japanese promise 1,125-line HDTV by way of DBS in Japan. It is possible that American cable systems could be upgraded to deliver the 1,125-line picture, a potential death blow to the broadcast TV industry.

One thing is already clear. The chances for a single world system are fast vanishing.

One could argue that the NHK initiative, clearly motivated by the needs of the world's primary professional television equipment manufacturing nation, has had the effect of promoting an overdue review of the quality of the television signal. Thus even if HDTV is not adopted it will have provoked a response which will benefit the public in the long term.

But the issue is really more fundamental. All the current HDTV and ACTV proposals are backward looking. They take, however unconsciously, the resolution of 35mm film as a benchmark. This width was established as the norm in Edison's lab in the late 1880s for the simple reason that Dickson (the assistant primarily responsible for the development of the kinetoscope) tried films of various widths in the course of his researches and settled on an image one inch wide as being the best (35mm equals one inch plus sprocket holes). It might be in some sense comforting to know that Japanese technicians in seeking to revolutionize the world's television have been trying to emulate Menlo Park. But is this the most rational basis upon which to move into the next century?

And this is without prejudice to handing the Japanese electronics industry a potential control, at the patent level, over the production of professional video equipment more complete than the one they currently exercise over consumer electronics. This control would be more complete because currently the basic patents relating to the dominant standards (for color, for instance) are not solely, or even, Japanese. Given the importance of these technologies to other fields, such as medicine and defense, such control would have ramifications well beyond the world of entertainment.

The French historian Fernand Braudel talks of societal "brakes" and "accelerators" working together to control the introduction of new technologies. The accelerators may be thought of as social needs or necessities. These take various forms. Needs can be created by other technologies, as the railways created the need for the telegraph or the deadnaught battleship for the radio. Non-technological social forces can be powerful accelerators. For instance, the rise of the nuclear family, the entertainment requirements of an urbanized population, the deep-seated and centuries-old cultural desire for realistic images would all be factors necessitating the development of television. Commercial considerations, like those that produced Super 8mm film or 8mm video or CDs, are also significant. I call these supervening social necessities.

"Brakes" can be thought of as those parallel social factors which slow the pace of diffusion and thus limit the potential of any new technology to disrupt existing social arrangements of all kinds, including, of course, the stability and health of companies. I like to describe these forces as a species of law—the "law" of the suppression of radical potential. This law states that new technologies are introduced into society only insofar as their radical potential for disrupting pre-existing social formations (in our society primarily of capital) is contained.

Both DAT and HD/ACTV are perfect examples of how the suppression of disruptive potential takes place. That the brakes are being applied to both these technologies does not mean that they will never see the light of day.

They will, almost certainly. But the brakes ensure that their diffusion will be controlled and hence their full potential will, perhaps, be distorted or never realized.

This vision is at some distance from the one offered by technological determinists, which assumes that technological change is a force in its own right and implies that it therefore cannot be easily controlled, contained, or regulated. The technological determinist rhetoric currently also claims that the pace of change is fast and getting faster. But, as the TVRO, DAT, and HD/ACTV examples suggest, there is reason for doubting such analyses.

For all of these advances, the social non-technological forces are paramount and the pace of the introduction of the technology is quite slow. This has always been true.

Television itself—that is, using a light-sensitive (photoemissive) material to translate an image into a modulated electrical current—was patented in 1884. The modern fully electronic TV system was a well-articulated idea by 1908. The first image was sent to a cathode ray tube in 1911. The basic patent for the camera was awarded in 1923.

In 1936, the FCC determined that RCA's system was not yet ready for the public. Yet that same year RCA television technology was being publicly used by both the Nazis and the British. The FCC's decision, although apparently determined by technological considerations, actually had more to do with the social ramifications of allowing RCA the unfettered exploitation of the advantage its patents had given it. It was to take five years to solve this problem. Then the second World War intervened.

But after the war, the FCC again moved to slow diffusion. Once more this action was taken in the name of technology—signal interference. The new TV signals were overlapping, but the FCC-imposed delay, which lasted no less than forty-three months, had profound effects on the nascent industry. Beneath the blanket created by the FCC "freeze," radio and film interests reached an accommodation over television which persists to this day. The three-network system was born. And the real technological issues of the time in television, color and a move to UHF, were solved by FCC action outside the "freeze."

The *de facto* suppression of television's radical potential over these decades allowed the maximum exploitation of talking pictures and radio, both of which might otherwise never have fully developed in the face of an early introduction of TV.

Such constraints on technological innovation do not need the action of regulators. The hidden hand will work as well, as the history of computing reveals. When the second World War ended, all computing activities began to close down. Nicholas Metropolis, a leading Los Alamos computing pioneer, returned to his university. Mauchly and Eckert, who had built ENIAC, nearly went bankrupt trying to find backers for their Electronic Control Company. Jay Forrester's team working on the first real-time computer at MIT was nearly disbanded.

It was the Russian A-bomb that brought all dying computer plans back to life. The device is a child of the hydrogen bomb partly because there was no rival supervening social necessity for the computer in the world of commerce. (The sophistication of the office machinery at this time is often forgotten.) The central role of the computer at the heart of the military industrial complex ensured that it remained an enormous, and enormously expensive, device. Its potential usefulness, in the form of a smaller, more manageable, more widely diffused machine was thus delayed for nearly thirty years. And in the late 1970s it was not the computer industry but fringe entrepreneurs who built the devices.

It will be objected that Wozniak and Jobs had, in solid state electronics, tools for miniaturization denied the pioneers. But the first computer to work in the world, in the summer of 1948, was designated the BABY MARK I. The history of computing is littered with discarded prototype micro machines, built, as was the BABY MARK I, to test a peripheral. The early computers were giants not because of tubes but because of Von Neumann. His prescriptive description of EDVAC (a widely circulated paper which contained the architecture of the first unequivocal stored program machine) called for a giant device specifically to work on nuclear problems. Nobody thought to build anything less for decades.

How can all these events, current and past, help us confront the challenge posed by the laser/fiber optics and establish an effective agenda for dealing with it?

We are witnessing the piecemeal substitution of the new technology for the old in the telephone system. In parallel to this, we have conducted long arguments about competition within that system and are currently debating whether or not to allow telephone interests to operate in cable television. The issues—fiber optics, inter-telco competition and telco/cable competition—are separate and, being separate, are a fertile ground for the suppression of the technology's potential. The effective rebuilding and consolidation of the infrastructure requires a far broader consideration than we are seeing. Piecemeal approaches are not likely to yield very efficient solutions.

It could be argued that in the matter of competition we are anyway reliving our own history. The debate about the break-up of AT&T took cognizance of the previous period of telephone competition, from the end of the Bell patents in 1894 until the nationalization experiment of 1918 and the legislation of 1921 (the Graham Act). The account given of that history in certain quarters, which found it to demonstrate the efficacy of competition, was tendentious. The nation's experience was that competitive telephony was counterproductive and duplicative. Today, as competitive trunklines are laid between major commercial centers and universal service takes a back seat to cream-skimming, the possibility that we will reach a conclusion similar to our grandparents' cannot be dismissed.

Some agenda which does not attempt to separate the technological from other issues ought to be sought.

The same broad integrative approach needs to be developed for international telecommunications issues. We have currently authorized transoceanic laser cable and an expansion of the space-side international communications system. This procedure might make market sense at an ideological level but it is, without question, contradictory. Here too we are revisiting the past.

Some historians argue that the possibility of using a U.S.-dominated space communications system as an instrument of foreign policy was well understood by President Johnson and his staffs. The British imperial cable system had survived the end of empire. To substitute a U.S. space system based on what was then a virtual U.S. monopoly in space would have been one of the more immediate and tangible pay-offs to the space race with the Soviets. Obviously the public announcement of this objective would have been extremely counterproductive, given the desire of nation states to maintain some sense of control over their international communications.

With this agenda hidden, the Congress then proceeded along other lines, to wit: the containment of the telephone company. The legislation (the Communications Satellite Act, 1962) did not allow AT&T into space but instead created another player, COMSAT. The chief characteristic of COMSAT was that it could be ignored by the Europeans, who continued to work with AT&T on the expansion of the transoceanic cable system. INTELSAT satellites (in which COMSAT represented the American interest) have been matched, step by step, with ever more capacious cables.

The satellites could do no more, most publicly in the area of international television transmissions, but America's trading partners, with more equal access to submarine wires, continued to refine that technology. AT&T remained a willing partner, and COMSAT's potential "imperial" role, if it can be so named, was nipped in the bud. In determining policy to contain AT&T in space, Congress caused the opportunity to remake the world's transoceanic communications system as an American preserve to be lost.

By the late 1990s the United States will have authorized at least one satellite communication company as a rival to COMSAT. That will break the international monopoly exercised by INTELSAT. But can this policy work in the face of the other authorization? New laser transoceanic cables could rapidly render all transoceanic satellites so much space junk.

Protecting national interests, especially in a period when easy technological leadership is not to hand, requires a more structured and long-term strategy than this.

In the matter of standards, consideration should be given to forcing the market to provide solutions above and beyond HDTV. Clearly the development of ACTV can proceed, subject to the usual and inevitable regulation of spectrum use. But the implications of the NHK system need to be very carefully examined. It could well be that HDTV as it is presently proposed represents the last grasp of Edison's 35mm image as a standard for the world. We might like to go beyond it.

We are not on a roller coaster of technological change. Technologies are developed and diffused at societies' behest. We are more than capable of taking control and determining the most effective and rational crucial next steps. A critical prerequisite to this is that the ideology of deregulation be abandoned; otherwise suitable "Communications for the Next Hundred Years" might prove elusive.

With the Mind's Eye . . .

KARL J. WEINTRAUB

Karl Weintraub, Thomas E. Donnelly Distinguished Service Professor at the University of Chicago, was born in Germany and grew up in Holland. In 1948, he came to the United States, where he earned bachelor's, master's, and Ph.D. degrees at the University of Chicago. In 1954, he joined the history faculty of his alma mater.

Besides serving through the years in such important administrative capacities as dean of the graduate division of the humanities, Professor Weintraub has achieved a reputation as a fine teacher, one who draws standing-room-only classes. His abilities have been recognized twice by the Quantrell Award for excellence in undergraduate teaching and by the Danforth Foundation.

As a scholar, Professor Weintraub acknowledges that he is "interested in things even historians aren't interested in!" The extensive list includes Western Civilization, modern European history, historiography, Holland in the seventeenth century, the history of autobiography, and the Baroque Age. Out of those interests have emerged his books: *Visions of Culture* (1966); *The Value of the Individual: Self and Circumstance in Autobiography* (1978); and *Essays on the Baroque* (1986).

YOU WILL HAVE ENOUGH experience with lectures to know that they are strange and unpredictable things. Some stranger stands before you with an announced title from which one does not know what to expect. I am especially aware of this because I have willfully decided to talk about a matter about which hardly anybody thinks much. It would surprise me if you do. But as an academic I believe, of course, that I may serve you best by trying to lead you away for a short while from all the things that are much on your mind. Whether this is fruitful, you must decide at the end. And if not, you may still have one reward: for any lecture can serve to teach us what we all have to learn and relearn constantly: namely, how to be bored with dignity.

Will you accept the proposition that human beings try to lead whole lives? All life long we seem to be engaged in arranging and rearranging the steady flow of impressions and of information and the knowledge we acquire. Inside of us we fashion patterns and coherences that tell something about us as persons and about the views of the world we have come to hold. In a process that is one of the great wonders of life, we form our personality, each and every one in a specific way. It seems altogether doubtful that we have fully come to understand this process. But it involves on one level the question of how we turn something knowable, coming to us from the outside, into inner and vital knowledge. For knowledge must somehow become our own, it must take on meaning for us, it must become a part of our living inner world to be effective in helping to form us as a person. As a historian, I have an interest in reflecting upon some of the ways by which we seem to form historical insights for ourselves. Taking from such reflections, I want to suggest something to you. And I hope that what seems to be a narrower professional concern indeed has much wider implications for our lives.

I want to ask some questions about some of the ways by which historical knowledge becomes a part of this inner world we seem to be forming. Our knowledge of the past, our very attitude toward the remembered past, toward our material and spiritual heritage, enter as much into this formation of ourselves and our corresponding worlds as all our other experiences, opinions, ideas, knowledge, fears, and aspirations. We are the animals with memory—just as much as we are the animals with imagination who project their hopes forward into the future. Our awareness, always in a momentary present, always has a forward-looking dimension of a present future, and a backward-looking dimension of a past that is now present for us. Whatever has taken shape in us as our own present past—which is, like all such things, a truly bewilderingly complex matter—functions as an important civilizing power in our lives. Without some sense of our past we are but barbarians.

No simple presentation can account adequately for the way by which knowledge of past things becomes a part of us. But let me sketch a limited aspect of this at least. One among the manifold ways by which we learn of things, by which we reason and gain insights and views from which we shape our inner worldview, concerns me in particular. Our eye is an especially powerful organ for coming to know the world around us. How important is the eye in forming our historical knowledge? On one level this is a very banal question. We obviously derive essential insights from seeing historical places, historical buildings, pictures, statues from former ages; we can visit ruins; we can even see mummies, old plows, and tools and artifacts *en masse*. Something different happens when playwrights render for us in visual presentations their conceptions of historical situations and personages, or when television treats us so very visually to the *Adams Chronicles*. All of this has importance for the formation of our historical views, but is not the matter that interests me here.

Most of what we know about the past—and that is true by a large measure—comes to us in the words of dead men. By far the greatest part of the past is not visually around us. You cannot simply be taken to it, to be shown what it concretely is. The basic material the historian has for somehow getting at the past consists of great and small fragments of statements left behind in words. From these the past must be reconstructed. And this reconstruction then comes to us again in terms of the words we read. Obviously we read these words with our eyes—but this banal matter is also not my concern. The real question I have is whether the eye plays a fundamental role in the knowledge of the past that comes to us through the words. Does the knowledge we obtain through words possess a strongly visual characteristic? Do we transpose words into pictures (a process which the Dutch can express so nicely in the simple verb *verbeelden*)? Do we have picture-forming, or "envisaging" habits? Do we—the beings with a past dimension—carry visions of past life within us?

Let me at least open up this issue by concentrating our attention for a while on an event from which we are quite far removed. Sometime in the year 481 or 480 B.C. a very large army of Persians and peoples subject to the Persian king, accompanied by a Phoenician fleet, at that time probably the largest in the world, was about to move into the mainland of Greece. With this powerful force the Persian King Xerxes meant to punish Greek city states that had supported fellow Greeks in Asia Minor who had rebelled against Persian rule. Ten years earlier the Athenians had beaten back an earlier Persian attack on Attica at Marathon. In order to get to the Greek mainland this huge army had to be moved across the Hellespont, or what we call the Dardanelles. Most of you may not think about these events at all any more; but I must scold you: that simply shows what awful historical ingrates you are! Actually this was one of those very great historical moments in the history of our Western world when our entire future was hanging in the balance. For if the Greeks had lost that struggle, we most likely would have an Oriental rather than a Western mentality. So every morning you should utter a little prayer of thanks for the victory at Salamis. But let that be! The one report we have of this moment is in Herodotus' *History of the Persian Wars*. When this immense Persian army—which he estimates at a million men—faced this great logistical maneuver of crossing the Hellespont, Herodotus makes a very interesting statement. He recounts how King Xerxes walks up onto a little elevation near the shore of Abydos, where the people of Abydos had built a marble seat for him. There he now surveys the entire scene. "When Xerxes saw the whole Hellespont hidden by his ships, and all the plains and shores of Abydos thronged with men, he first praised himself a happy man, and presently fell aweeping."

Now what happens when we let this scene work on us? Let us try to open ourselves up and somehow experience this scene; let us make it something we somehow wish to possess. Whenever we approach the past in a receptive mood, then the few remnants from the past—a few bars of an old song, the fleeting impression of a painting, a few words—may touch off an awareness in us of a past reality. Wilhelm von Humboldt called this *ein Ahnen*, a vague surmising, a subtle apperception of something we had not noticed before. It results from the most basic historical instinct: namely, to let the past into our lives. This form of historical sensation involves us in the process whereby we, gradually or suddenly, become aware of the shapes and forms of former things that are past but not so lost that they cannot be reconstructed. What then occurs is a resurrection before the mind's eye. We have fleeting impressions as if in the sphere of a dream. It is like a seeing of untouchable figures, a hearing of half-heard words. Hippolyte Taine said that history was an "approximate seeing of men of former times"—"*L'histoire c'est à peu près voir les hommes d'autrefois*," a phrase in which one had better not overlook the *à peu près*. It can only be an approximate seeing. The mind's eye sees, but it is only a vision with shadows, only a reconstruction "by the moonlight of memory."

Herodotus gives us only a limited description in the sentence beginning "And when Xerxes saw the whole Hellespont." Yet the more we open up our inner senses to the scene and let it enjoy our attention, the more this scene begins to fill out. There is a man on some elevation from which an ordered landscape opens out. He, and we, see water and ships, a coastline and men on the land. There are visual lines in all of this, a foreground, a background; there is an arrangement of subordinated and of dominant parts of the view. And there are things that Herodotus does not mention at all: there is sky, there is the medium of air, which conditions the perspective into the distance, and there is light in which the scene is embedded. By and by we may perceive the ships as certain clusters, the shoreline with bays and jutting promontories. The men appear to be in groups, they take on clearer forms, and they may be moving and acting as soldiers do when they are in bivouac. The longer the mind's eye dwells on the scene, the more the scene comes alive, the more details emerge in the total image that Herodotus only sketched in half a sentence.

Our picture-forming mind, our image-forming inner eye adds data that the historical source has not given us. Is this responsible? Does the mind have a right to do this? We feel uneasy about it. We could of course tell ourselves: "Let us stick just to what the historian has given us; to more we have no right. So, let us move on to the next scene he does give us." But by doing that, we cut ourselves off from the experience of the past we sought to possess in the first place. After all, the urge to enter into that historical moment, to touch upon another life, a past life, this urge can be very genuine. It originates in a very deep and very noble instinct: to be in touch with mankind in its full richness, its misery, and its manifold splendor. So, it seems that something drives us to that scene. And if we stay with such a scene, we will be inevitably immersed in a process of filling in, of rounding off, of deepening the mere outlines. Insofar as the mind has this image-forming habit, how do we call a stop to it? Our experience of all reality is so strongly visual, how can we avoid allowing our reconstruction of past reality to assume a kind of visual concreteness? The mind's eye does not seem to have the eyelid that the outer eye can use to shut out imposing reality.

And yet this actively roving inner eye, this visualizing inner eye, is being restrained by a harsh historical conscience. Clearly, the historian is not permitted to invent as freely as the poet may. The historian's data, his sources set strict limits to his imagination; they are something binding. And the historian fears the sin of anachronism: misplacing things in time. Our aversion to this sin warns us that we cannot clothe these Persian soldiers in G.I. uniforms, or think of those ships in modern form. We can make the very basic correction of reading the passage in the original Greek so that our English words are not misleading us. We know that we can appease that historical conscience only by coming to see fifth-century realities with fifth-century eyes. We have to ask, What did Persian costumes look like? How would Phoenician ships have appeared from some distance? How wide is the Hellespont? What sort of plant life was likely to grow near Abydos? What did a royal Persian face look like? Many of these corrections we can make by trying to find out. And this search can get to be pretty sophisticated: for instance, we may go to Abydos and study its shoreline and even make the correction for the way in which the unceasing work of the waves over many centuries may have altered that coast. At closer inspection, therefore, it appears that there are many powerful means whereby we also discipline this inner process of visualizing a world. This matter depends upon one's commitment to intellectual honesty.

But however much we may discipline the imaginative process by ministering to facts and reliable knowledge, some uncontrollable personal (if you prefer: subjective) elements are going to fashion the inner vision of the past we are forming. Even if I have made all the laudable efforts to find out as much as I can about every detail of the scene, making all the refined checks and corrections possible, I may still add things that simply cannot be confirmed. Suppose no evidence exists about meteorological conditions. We cannot envisage landscapes without weather. And nothing will prevent one mind from seeing the scene bathed in bright sunlight with glorious reflections of white sails on the softly curling waves, or another from seeing it through a light haze and the ships in the shadow of billowing clouds. And if we are observant, we notice that numerous details in the arrangement of the scene similarly depend on very personal choices. As we begin to live with that past moment, as we learn to see and to walk and to smell and to hear in that historical landscape, we fashion in very subtle ways a vision that is a wondrous composite of hard facts and imagination.

Something very similar occurs as we now try to understand the startling sensations of Xerxes, the king, who "first declared himself happy, and presently fell aweeping." What is going on inside him? Why does the joy turn into tears? Obviously he is elated by what he sees, and just as obviously he is being haunted by some misgiving. Or is he one of those persons whom too strong elation always moves to tears? If we make the effort to find out everything Herodotus has told us about the man in earlier passages, we may remember him as a very proud man, proud of the achievements of his race and his great forefathers, easily irritated by such upstarts as these Greeks who try to thwart his ambition to rule. He is a man with a temper who became so furious at the waves of the Hellespont when they destroyed the first bridge built across it, that he ordered the sea flogged. But he is also sensitively aware of his earlier dreams and his uncle's warning about the unpredictability of fortune; and he knows that his father's expedition against these Greeks ended in the disaster at Marathon a decade earlier. So, here he is: possessed of this immense army, this enormous instrument of power, which nothing will be able to resist, assuring his glory as the greatest of all Persians, and yet he is overcome with sadness about the caducity of human life, fearing the death so many of his brave ones will have to suffer. And here we stand as historians, a bit like Odysseus in Hades wanting to speak again with past comrades, who cannot speak to him unless he slaughters an ox so that the mere shades may drink the blood, let it course through them, and thus be revived for a short while for a common meeting—except that we do not slaughter the ox but pour our own life blood, our feelings, thoughts, and imagination into the shades from the past so that they may communicate with us for a fleeting moment.

If we have lived with this scene for a while in the right way we may be astonished how the barely alive words of Herodotus have evolved for us into a wondrously rich inner vision. Somehow, in our present, we seem to participate with past actors in extraordinary adventures. And if we wish to follow them from the Hellespont we can forever enrich the vision by incorporating more actors and different landscapes and further adventures, until we have arranged them all in an ever widening and deepening tableau that contains for our inner viewing the whole struggle between Persians and Greeks, the victory of the Greeks, their subsequent glories in sculpture, a Parthenon, Sophocles and Aristophanes, Socrates and Plato, and even those later Roman friends who transmitted so much of this knowledge of the Greeks to our own tradition. We have linked ourselves to the past, and something of it now seems to be actively living in us. The animal with memory, feeding the mind's eye with rich visions, has indeed wondrous experiences.

Some of you will say: "But so often history is not being given to us in such graphic concreteness." That is correct. Much of our modern historical writing presents insights about the past in terms of great abstractions; often it deals with human masses from which hardly a single individual stands out; it deals with institutional patterns, voting behavior, unfathomable economic forces, and large cultural configurations intersected by complicated networks of human activity. Much of it comes in numbers, and numbers do not lend themselves to the forming of inner pictures. The reasons for this are understandable on one level. Our great masses of historical data have to be ordered and probed in many different fashions for fresh insights and deeper understanding. On another level this change in historical style is the sad consequence of the professionalization of history. Most modern historians write for fellow historians and not the general public (whom they often surrender to the quacks who love to titillate with the sensational stuff only). Test sometime how many so-called history books simply assume that the reader knows the basic story on which all that sophisticated generalization is based.

But when all is said and done, the human story about the past is the fundamental bedrock for our knowledge of it and our real point of contact with it. And the story must involve the human being as the point of historical fascination, as its actor doing, thinking, feeling, dreaming, wishing, suffering, and glorying in its existence. Institutions, states, economies, have no history; human beings who express their lives in part by working through such agencies have histories, individually and in groups. In the last analysis we come back to this intriguing question—

how a process of disciplined imagination can put us in touch with a vast world of dead people.

As our preoccupation with the scene of Xerxes at the Hellespont makes eminently clear, our wish to possess the past moment starts with a dilemma. Strictly speaking, there is no historical landscape there; there is no external tableau that is simply reflected in the mirror of our mind. There is no discernible order of a past out there that can simply be "uncovered" (by means of what the Greeks called *aletheia*, a process of uncovering the truth); there is no form out there that impresses itself on the mind like a seal on a wax tablet. There are only bits and pieces of data, mainly some words. (And it really would not be essentially different if there were a drawing or some pictorial form.) There are some remnants—be they words, pictures, artifacts, musical notes, or archaeological remains—that are evidence of a past reality. The "something" wanted by the historical instinct, by the historical quest, lies behind this evidence. We have to probe for it. We have to recreate it, to re-experience it, to re-endow it with some semblance of life. And the more graphically concrete we can make this for ourselves, the better. That past also is entitled to its warm glow and its distinctiveness. For in a deep sense this activity, this quest is haunted and is being fed by our conviction that these human beings back there were once as real and as alive as most of us. The sun was shining in their lives, the rains fell on them, they knew hunger and love and fear; their surroundings had their own colors.

Out of such fragments of revived life larger views of a whole are by and by being composed by the historian, be he professional or amateur (if it were not such an ugly phrase, I would be inclined to say by the historicizing person). In composing the larger views, the historian selects what he considers relevant and characteristic in terms of his growing vision. According to his growing judgment, he arranges images into larger tableaux in terms of what fits. He constructs the larger views by establishing meaningful relations among the sub-parts. He determines what goes into the foreground and what goes into the background, on what the light falls and what stays in the half-light. There cannot be any doubt that this process is full of dangers and that some horrible intellectual crimes can be committed in this way. And yet it may be more important still that one start this process sometime, somewhere, somehow, with something. As one becomes charmed by it, one may gradually learn how to refine it, how to guard at least against unnecessary falsification, and how to do it with growing refinement and intellectual responsibility. Even in a lifetime of careful training, however, the historian will recognize that he is primarily guided in his activity by his sense of responsibility toward past life that wants to be accepted on its own terms; he is guided by an unwillingness to falsify knowingly, a deep urge to give meaning to the fragments of the past by using his most refined sense of what is plausible about the human existence, and by a mysteriously growing sense of what fits and what belongs. To wrestle with the angel is our human destiny; we will never win. Knowing that all of this is imperfect knowledge is the best thing for preserving our sense of proportion and our intellectual modesty.

The story about the historian I have started does not quite end there. A very complicated issue comes into play once the historian has formed before his mind's eye a fuller vision of the historical matter he wishes to understand. It lives before his mind's eye—but for him alone. He can carry this vision to his grave, as we all do with most of our understanding of the world that we have formed so slowly and at such psychic costs. Or he can try to share his vision with some others at least. And then he faces an interesting task. He must communicate images, pictures that are only in his mind. And how shall he do this?

Much of what I have said may have left the expectation that I would favor using the pictorial arts for communicating the historical visions in the historian's mind: make picture books, make movies, present as much as possible in historical museum displays. But that is not at all what I favor. The fixed picture is static—and this presents great difficulties for imagining matters that are fluctuating and in motion. If you are interested in this matter, study Lessing's *Laokoon* again. The picture and the moving picture give much too sharp and too concrete an outline to visions of the mind that never can have that same sharpness of contour and brightness of color. We even have that problem when great drama is being turned into a movie for us. For our aesthetic experience it is an altogether different matter whether we hear from an actor on stage the queen's account of Ophelia's death or see it in Lawrence Olivier's version of *Hamlet* on celluloid. Says the queen:

> There is a willow grows aslant a brook
> That shows his hoar leaves in the glassy stream;
> There with phantastic garlands she did come
> Of crow-flowers, nettles, daisies, and long purples
> That liberal shepherds give a grosser name,
> But our cold maids do dead men's fingers call them;
> There, on the pendent boughs her coronet weeds
> Clamb'ring to hang, an envious sliver broke;
> When down her weedy trophies and herself
> Fell in the weeping brook. Her clothes spread wide,
> And, mermaid-like, awhile they bore her up;
> Which time she chanted snatches of old tunes,
> As one incapable of her own distress,
> Or like a creature native and indued
> Unto that element: but long it could not be
> Till that her garments, heavy with their drink,
> Pull'd the poor wretch from her melodious lay
> To muddy death.

Laertes: Alas, then she is drowned?
    Drown'd, drown'd.
                                        (IV. vii. 167–85)

Do you really want to have the concrete picture of her wreath floating off on the gurgling brook, as the filmmaker presented it? The problem with the historical picture is a very analogous matter. As the great Dutch historian, Johan Huizinga, whose work inspired many of these reflections for me, very wisely said, historical reconstruction occurs by the dimmer moonlight of memory. And he also suggested that the historical view of anything is always "an open context"; it must not be closed off, it must be receptive to subtle modifications as the view and the perspective shift. The word, written or spoken, preserves for us this open context. It is therefore desirable and fortunate that the historian rely on literary means for communicating his vision. He must learn to practice the art of ecphrasis—the art of expressing images in words. He must be able to translate his visions into words that can evoke images again in the mind of the reader. He should follow the old advice of Erasmus when that wise humanist tried to teach others how to write: "Set it up like a picture to look at, so that we seem to have painted the scene rather than described it, and the reader seems to have seen rather than have read." When you think about it, it is really a very complicated art and a wonderfully perplexing process. By choosing the right descriptive words and by being very economical about it so that the receiver need not think things away again that should not be there, the images before one mind's eye have to be transferred to another's mind's eye, preferably without loss in content or meaning. The difficulty of this process also makes great historians very rare. But when it works it can be very good.

Let me give you two examples on which you can try whether it works. One comes from Jacob Burckhardt's *Greek Cultural History*. After having described how Alexander the Great with his Macedonians and Greeks has completely defeated the Persians at Gaugamela in 333 B.C., the beginning of that great melting of Greek civilization with the rich resources of Eastern worlds into the Hellenistic world, he relates that Alexander entered the conquered tent of Darius and found there an extremely precious jewel chest. "He placed a manuscript of the *Iliad* in the magnificent jewelled chest which became his booty with Darius' splendid tent; thus it happened literally: Hellenic spirit was to be framed in oriental riches." Or another one from Huizinga's opening chapter of *The Waning of the Middle Ages:*

> Then, again all things in life were of a proud or cruel publicity. Lepers sounded their rattles and went about in processions, beggars exhibited their deformity and their misery in churches. Every order and estate, every rank and profession, was distinguished by its costume. The great lords never moved about without a glorious display of arms and liveries, exciting fear and envy. Executions and other public acts of justice, hawking, marriages and funerals, were all announced by cries and processions, songs and music. The lover wore the colors of his lady; companions the emblem of their fraternities; parties and servants the badges and blazons of their masters. . . . A medieval town did not lose itself in extensive suburbs . . . and villas; girded by its walls, it stood forth as a compact whole, bristling with innumerable turrets. However tall and threatening the houses of noblemen or merchants might be, in the aspect of the town the lofty mass of the churches always dominated. . . . One sound rose ceaselessly above the noises of busy life and lifted all things unto a sphere of order and serenity: the sound of bells.

The world and the practices of the historian may not be your cup of tea. If so, I apologize for trying to pull you to it. But if you have followed what I tried to say, you will have concluded that the historian's ways are in no way exceptional. We all form our inner worlds in very similar ways. The external world enters us constantly, and so much through the eye; we read novels, we listen, we absorb. And out of all of this we secretly select what is important and meaningful for us, we order this and we form larger more coherent inner visions of the world and human life within it. And much of this is an internal way of seeing. And the richness of life we possess depends on the richness, the fullness, the liveliness of our vision. It might be worthwhile to think about this at times. And it might be rewarding to think about and to practice the art of ecphrasis, the ability to transfer our insights to others. For we can either carry all this inner treasure of views silently to the grave—as we do with most of it, for sure—or try to share the best of it.

National Service in America: An Idea Whose Time Is Coming

CHARLES C. MOSKOS

Charles Moskos, professor and chairperson of the Department of Sociology at Northwestern University, attended Princeton University, where he received his B.A. *cum laude* in 1956. After military service in the U.S. Army combat engineers, he studied at the University of California at Los Angeles, earning master's and Ph.D degrees.

Dr. Moskos is the author of many books and monographs, including *The American Enlisted Man, Public Opinion and the Military Establishment,* and *The Modern Military—More Than Just a Job?.* In addition to more than one hundred articles in scholarly journals, he has published pieces in the *New York Times,* the *Washington Post,* the *Wilson Quarterly,* the *Atlantic,* and *Foreign Affairs.*

A leading figure in the study of military sociology, Dr. Moskos often spends time living with service members. His research has taken him to army units in Vietnam, the Dominican Republic, Korea, Germany, and Honduras; navy ships in the Atlantic; and air force missions in the Pacific. Dr. Moskos is frequently called upon to testify before Congress as an expert witness on military manpower and youth service issues.

N<small>O MORE POWERFUL EXPRESSION</small> of civic duty exists than what is commonly called "national service." This entails the full-time undertaking of public duties by young people—whether as citizen soldiers or civilian servers—who are paid subsistence wages. *National* is used here in the broadest sense. It encompasses youth service performed at the state, local, and community levels for both governmental agencies and nonprofit organizations. Common to all such service is the performance of socially needed tasks that the market cannot effectively handle and that would be too expensive for government employees to carry out.

From the beginning, it is important to understand that national service must not be seen as a magical talisman, a mystical means for transforming socially indifferent Americans into paragons of civic virtue. But national service does mean the performance of citizen duties that allow individuals to have a sense of the civic whole—a whole that is more important than any single person or category of persons. It is upon some such norm of fulfillment of a civic obligation, upon some concept of serving societal needs outside the marketplace, upon some sense of participation in a public life with other citizens that the idea of national service builds. We will refer to these notions, for purpose of shorthand, as *civic content*.

Confusion among national service supporters about who is supposed to benefit from the work performed—the server or society—has produced two schools of thought about national service, what might be called the *instrumental* and the *civic*. The instrumental tradition justifies national service by the good done to the server. The civic tradition focuses on the value of the services performed. The first tradition provokes negative stereotypes by inviting speculation on deficiencies in the character of the server. The second tradition offers national service as an end in itself, thereby fostering positive images of servers. Only when national service is cast in terms of its civic content can its positive, but necessarily derivative, benefits for the server be achieved.

For good reasons national service is almost always presented as a program for youth. Although arrangements can be made for older people to participate in national-service programs, the primary focus must be on teenagers and young adults. From a practical point of view, young people are more flexible than adults and have fewer family obligations. Furthermore, since many have not yet entered the work force, young participants would prove less disruptive to the nation's economy; indeed, their value as workers may be enhanced by the service experience itself, thereby making America more competitive in the new realities of global economic interdependence. In addition, young adults can usually perform certain physical tasks—notably military and conservation work—more efficiently than older people. The growing tendency of American youth to postpone the responsibilities of adulthood makes national service potentially an attractive way-station between school and work. But there is also an intangible: focusing national service on youth makes it a rite of passage toward adult citizenship, dramatizing its importance.

One other issue must be gotten out of the way. Because civic content is the lodestone of national service, whether the service performed is compulsory or voluntary is not an essential element of any definition of national service, however profound may be the policy implications of that question. I will propose a form of comprehensive national service that would include a substantial number of youth—as many as one million in either military or civilian service—and that would not be mandatory. By promoting a spirit of civic-mindedness, national service will accomplish a range of much needed national tasks, thus reshaping American life in fundamental ways.

The Comparable Worth of Military and Civilian Service

Support for national service usually divides into two very distinct schools. One, the tough-minded, is concerned primarily with military manpower. The second, the high-minded, defines national service in civilian terms. The fundamental philosophical question is whether military and civilian service are close together or poles apart. The short answer is that they are both. My argument is that the opposition between the tough-minded and high-minded approaches to national service is resolvable and is even mutually reinforcing once the two are joined under the banner of civic duty. Military and civilian service, if not quite a seamless web, are, to the degree they contain civic content, cut out of the same cloth.

On the whole, the supporters of civilian and military service have much more in common than they realize. Both parties agree that national service must stand apart from marketplace considerations. Both call for the participation of a large cross section of American youth. Both believe that society is served by fostering in young people a commitment to citizen duties. Only by drawing on both tough-minded and high-minded wellsprings can national service ever hope to become a reality.

Some dozen bills were introduced in the 100th Congress proposing forms of national service for youth. It would take us far afield to describe each of these, but suffice it to say that the common thread in the proposed legislation is the question of the comparable worth of military and civilian service. The reality is that there is no simple or elegant way to measure comparable worth of citizen soldiers and civilian servers. To assert as I do that civic content underpins all forms of national service does not mean that all require equal sacrifice. I think it can be safely said, however, that military service is inherently more dangerous than most forms of civilian service and therefore deserves greater weight in any assessment of duties. This point of view almost surely corresponds to the folk understanding of the relative onerousness of military and civilian service.

This observation brings us back to the central point: military and civilian service may have incommensurate worth, but they both entail the performance of civic duties. From this perspective, the citizen soldier has more in common with the conscientious objector performing alternative service than with the vocal patriot who has managed legally to avoid the draft. The Peace Corps volunteer shares more in common with the draftee than with the political radical who views all service for the American state as an exercise in imperialism. Both citizen soldiers and civilian servers display a commitment to undertaking the duties of citizenship: both have agreed to spend a period of their lives for a civic purpose that is not going to be a lifetime career; both, for the common good, have temporarily stepped outside the cash-work nexus of the marketplace.

In sum, although it is worth acknowledging the differences between military and civilian service, we ought not to press the point too hard. To argue as I have that both have a shared civic content can take us only so far: a long way to be sure, but not the whole distance. Ultimately, we must be a little inconsistent. Although we cannot be unaware of the differences between military and civilian service, we need not always recognize them; better to keep our eye on the civic commonalities. Accordingly, the proposals given below offer both citizen soldier and civilian service options for American youth.

Reconstruction of the Citizen Soldier

Beginning in 1973, the United States sought to accomplish something it had never before attempted—to maintain a huge active-duty and reserve military force on a strictly voluntary basis. The effort has met with mixed reviews. The All-Volunteer Force (AVF) has been analyzed, dissected, and critiqued in an endless stream of books, reports, articles, and congressional hearings. In brief, the 1970s were a period of extreme difficulty in recruiting the required numbers and quality of soldiers, whereas the 1980s have witnessed a sharp change for the better.

The architects of the AVF saw large pay raises for lower-ranking personnel as the principal means to induce persons to join the AVF. The real income of recruits is now double what it was during the peacetime draft. By 1987, a private first class earned the equivalent of $16,000—a salary approximating the average starting wage for a teacher in America. A look at some dollar figures (presented in constant 1986 values) gives us a sense of the change in the military budget since the peacetime-draft years. In 1964, the total manpower bill came to not quite $84 billion; in 1986, the total was $117 billion. In other words, we are now spending $33 billion more a year for manpower costs than during the draft, even though we have a half million fewer soldiers (2.6 million in 1964, 2.1 million in 1987) on active duty.

The improved recruiting picture that started in the early 1980s resulted from the convergence of several key developments—a high youth unemployment rate, a significant rise in military pay, and, more intangibly, a waning of the antimilitary sentiments generated by the Vietnam War. But the army's successful enlistment record also owed much to the discernment of a recruit pool not moved by high pay and cash bonuses. With the introduction of short two-year enlistments and post-service educational benefits in the form of a new GI Bill, a college-bound youth population was attracted into the military. The success of these recruitment incentives is the starting point for the concept of the citizen soldier in the AVF.

The armed forces need to recognize the difference between those who might see the military as a hiatus in their lives and those who might make a long-term career commitment to the armed forces. The army can set up a two-track system accommodating both the citizen soldier and the professional soldier. The professional soldier will be the same kind of soldier recruited under the status quo; such professionals, with their long initial enlistments, will be the primary recipients of the advanced training required for a technical military force.

In contrast to the professional soldier, the citizen soldier would serve a short term, two years at the most (the term of the old draftee), or a six-month term of training followed by a reserve obligation. Citizen soldiers would generally be given the kinds of assignments—in the combat arms, for example—that were formerly filled by draftees. These are the areas in today's military where recruitment shortfalls and premature attrition are most likely to occur. Active-duty pay for the citizen soldier would be lower—say, by one third—than that received by the professional soldier of the same rank. Of the approximately 400,000 enlisted positions that AVF must recruit annually, at least a quarter could be adequately filled by citizen soldiers.

The central proposal for reintroducing the citizen soldier in the AVF is a generous GI Bill package of post-service educational benefits. The actual dollar figures of a GI Bill are subject to modification, but my proposal is for a $24,000 maximum award for the two-year enlistee and a $12,000 entitlement for the reserve enlistee. For a GI Bill to be truly cost-effective and attract really new recruits into the armed forces, it must be linked to the low-pay, short-enlistment option outlined above. Connecting GI Bill eligibility with a citizen-soldier option would help attract those young people for whom high recruit pay or enlistment bonuses are insufficient inducements; moreover, the low-pay feature would minimize the siphoning off of those already predisposed to join the military.

The challenge facing the AVF is to find an equivalent of the peacetime draftee. Rather than looking backward toward conscription, we ought to look forward to a state of affairs in which the model of the citizen soldier can be subsumed within a broader concept of comprehensive citizenship obligation. A growing expectation of national service among young people generally will improve the climate of military recruitment without resort to ever-higher compensation for the recruits or ever-higher reliance on career soldiers. If the AVF is to survive, it must reach the largely untapped pool of talented and upwardly mobile youth who would find a temporary diversion from the world of work or school tolerable, and perhaps even welcome.

A Practical Proposal for Civilian Service

Any practical proposal for national service must take into account some basic features of the national mood. Many Americans seem convinced that our society is rapidly losing its civic consciousness, one important result being that important social needs are going unmet. At the same time, the public does not seem prepared to support any program that would be compulsory or would require the creation of a huge bureaucracy. Building on such sentiments, a successful national-service program would have to be both voluntary and comprehensive; it should be neither federal nor local but something of both. My proposal would involve about one million young people a year; about 400,000 would join the military (100,000 as citizen soldiers) as outlined above, and another 600,000 would enter civilian service.

For any civilian-service program to succeed, it must perform work that otherwise would remain undone because there is no profit in it for the private sector and because the public sector cannot afford it. If a national-service program cannot provide services more effectively or more cheaply than private enterprise or employees of public agencies, then there is no basis for it. A partial listing of specific tasks is

> education—tutors, teachers' aides
> health care—aides for inpatient care in hospitals, nursing homes, hospices, mental institutions, providers of home care and transportation services for the aged and handicapped
> child care—workers for home care, center-based care, and care in work sites
> conservation—forestry planting, soil conservation, construction and maintenance in recreation areas
> justice—police reserves, civilian patrols, police staff support
> libraries and museums—preservers of books and collections.

National servers would receive a stipend, say $100 weekly, along with health and life insurance; room and board would be provided if need be with corresponding reductions in the stipend. The normal workweek would be forty hours. The basic length of service would be one year. The core compensation would be in the form of post-service educational and job-training benefits. A civilian GI Bill would be introduced offering the enrollee $10,000 in post-benefits. The long-term goal is that only national servers would be eligible for federal educational benefits. This is to say that the current $9 billion expended annually on federal aid to college students would in time do double duty: broadening access to higher education and rewarding civilian servers.

Administering the program would be a Corporation for National Youth Service. It would function as a public corporation in the mold of the Corporation for Public Broadcasting. The president and Congress would jointly appoint the board. Congress would appropriate funds for the corporation, which would then award grants to state and local youth corps. The corporation would also coordinate programs administered by federal agencies, serve as a clearinghouse for national-service initiatives, and have a small research staff. The corporation itself would not directly supervise national servers or carry out national-service functions.

The goal is to have the great majority of civilian youth serve outside the federal realm. Most activity would occur at the state and local levels. Nonprofit service organizations must play a critical role in any comprehensive national-service program, since these organizations are typically labor-intensive and have a constant problem affording nonspecialized help. To ensure that youth servers would perform useful roles, a cost-sharing mechanism would be introduced by all agencies that participate in the national-service program.

It is difficult to be precise about the costs of national service. But from the record of past and present youth-service projects, there is reasonable consensus on the factors affecting costs. But any large-scale program will cost money, and it is best to say so up front. The key variables are the amount of compensation per enrollee, the level of staffing, the ratio of residential to nonresidential participants, administration, and postservice benefits. The benchmark estimates are $9,000 per slot in a nonresidential program (the average cost per VISTA volunteer) to about $16,000 for a residential program (the per-enrollee cost of the Job Corps). In broad terms, a program of 600,000 civilian servers would come to about $7 billion a year.

To be really complete, a budgeting exercise on national service must include the value of the work performed. What is the final value of preserving our physical resources, cleaning up our environment, caring for the elderly and handicapped, rescuing our research collections, staffing our public institutions with servers, and opening up new avenues for dead-end youth? There is no ready answer. Even though evaluation studies of service programs indicate that for every dollar expended at least one dollar of value is gained, such studies can go only so far. By focusing on either short-term impacts on program participants or economic analyses of specific services delivered, evaluation researchers typically fail to include the more general societal benefits that a national-service program would provide. The gains in civic culture and social consensus, though difficult to measure, would surely be sizeable.

For and Against National Service

Many arguments have been advanced against national service. Here are a half-dozen of the most serious, in ascending order of difficulty: (1) national service would displace gainfully employed workers; (2) it would be difficult to find useful work for national servers; (3) national-service work could be better performed by the market; (4) national service would merely be a cover for a compulsory youth program or a military draft; (5) costs for a national-service system would be astronomical and its administration hopelessly complex; and (6) unless national service is universal, it would aggravate already existing divisions in American society.

In responding to these objections, my intention is not to defend all types of national service but rather to keep the argument focused on the program I have proposed, a comprehensive, noncompulsory program embracing both civilian servers and a citizen soldiery.

On the issue of job displacement, there is only one acceptable rejoinder: national service must be restricted to work that otherwise would not be performed. The whole rationale for national service is that it meets needs currently filled by neither the marketplace nor the government. A 1986 study by the Ford Foundation calculated that there exist 3.5 million jobs now being performed that nonspecialized one-year servers could fill. Surely, then, a program involving 600,000 civilian slots could be managed so as to have a minimal effect on the regular workforce.

At bottom, the labor-substitution issue is more a political problem than anything else. For this reason, it is essential that organized labor be represented on administrative boards at the national, state, and local levels. Much as Franklin D. Roosevelt defused labor opposition to the Civilian Conservation Corps by appointing a labor leader to head it, labor must be allotted a substantial policymaking role in a national-service program. In an important sense, a national-service system could even help labor; for, by reducing unemployment, it would tighten the labor market, thereby enhancing union bargaining power in the long term.

A second argument against national service is, ironically, a partial contradiction of the first. Many detractors maintain that work in national service does not lead to "real" jobs. Such a complaint reflects a basic misconception about national service. It is not a jobs program and should never be defined as such. National service is rather performance of work as a citizenship duty, work of high priority that would otherwise not get done. As I have tried to show, national service benefits its participants most when it is not defined as a jobs program. Work discipline, personal maturity, self-reliance, participation in a common civic enterprise—these are the qualities that help a person find a job, and national service can play an important role in inculcating them. In this sense, civilian service could extend the character-building role often performed by the military.

A third objection is that national-service work could be more efficiently performed if left to the market. This view grows out of the conservative conviction that even the best-intentioned intervention in the marketplace usually produces negative results. This is not a frivolous argument. But again, this perspective ignores the purpose of national service, which is to perform work neglected by the marketplace as well as by the government. National service is especially suited for work that can be done by nonspecialized workers. Indeed, to the degree that many human services—care for the infirm, aged, and mentally ill comes quickly to mind—require menial labor combined with compassion, short-term servers are better suited for them than the high-turnover, alienated workers who too often perform these tasks today, if they are performed at all.

A fourth argument against national service is that even a voluntary program would inevitably turn compulsory. This is a natural fear, especially when the system being proposed offers strong inducements—postservice educational and job-training benefits—to national servers that are not available (or are much restricted) to those youth who have not served. I find singularly unpersuasive the view that only those who serve without any reward are truly worthy of being called national servers. Only the extraordinarily idealistic (or perhaps neurotic) would serve without any recompense whatsoever. Thus, I have unabashedly constructed a program that rewards those who serve their country or community more than those who do not. But the transition from the voluntary system proposed here to a compulsory program would certainly be a momentous step—one that simply could come about without widespread support. And, needless to say, such support would exist only if the voluntary program were widely viewed as a great success. It seems perverse, then, to argue against a voluntary national scheme on the grounds that it might prove too successful.

More to the point, perhaps, is the objection that a comprehensive national-service program could serve as a cover for reinstating a military draft. Indeed it might. But it is virtually unimaginable that a compulsory civilian program would be legislated (even presuming constitutional obstacles could somehow be overcome) prior to enactment of military conscription. If the draft were to come back, however, the prior existence of a voluntary system would surely create strong pressures to make the program compulsory, for men certainly, for women probably. But it seems silly to argue that any form of national service should be avoided simply because it might make a draft more palatable. Surely, a palatable draft is better than an unpalatable one. Again, the possible success of a program ought not be used as an argument against it.

A fifth source of opposition to national service is found among critics who concentrate on administrative and budgetary problems. Certainly a mandatory program involving millions of young people could become a bureaucratic and financial nightmare. But the plan advanced here envisions a highly streamlined administration. Citizen soldiers would be absorbed into the existing armed forces with a minimum of organizational adjustment. Most civilian servers, too, would be assigned to existing institutions—nonprofit organizations, schools, hospitals, and government agencies. Of the remainder, nearly all would serve in conservation corps for which there is already extensive organizational experience allowing for ready expansion with economies of scale. The key is decentralization. Any scheme that would seek to impose a uniform system on a country as large and diverse as America would probably collapse of its own weight.

Nonetheless, it must be acknowledged that comprehensive national service will not come cheap. The outlays are substantial, and there is no getting around that fact. But it is important to keep the cost issue in perspective. During the peak years of the World War II GI Bill, benefits came to almost 1 percent of the gross national product—about $45 billion in today's economy. The $7 billion in new federal funds that a national-service program would require represents less than a sixth of the initial GI Bill.

The most damaging objection to national service is, ironically, the one that opponents are least likely to mention, perhaps because they view it less as a drawback than a saving grace. I refer to the possibility that national service could replicate—if not exacerbate—the class and racial divisions within American society. Whatever the legal and practical questions about compulsory service, there is one powerful argument in its favor—social equity. What must be kept in mind, however, is that the comprehensive program that I have outlined is much more inclusive than any other voluntary program ever put forth. Also, my linchpin proposal to give priority, and eventually sole eligibility, for postsecondary school benefits to national servers is a qualitative leap from any other volunteer scheme.

The critical point is that sharing the obligations of citizenship will act as a solvent for most of the differences among the various kinds of national servers. That all participants will be living at subsistence levels and that all will be eligible for postservice benefits underscore the egalitarianism of the national-service program. Precisely because large numbers of youth from across the social spectrum would participate—if not shoulder-to-shoulder, then under one large umbrella—invidious stereotyping would be kept to a minimum, bringing about much the same leveling effect that has traditionally occurred among members of the military services.

Making National Service a Reality

The obstacles in the way of national service are considerable. I see three scenarios, not in any way exclusive of each other, by which national service can come into being. One is through the return of a military draft—a development that would surely create pressures for creating some form of alternative civilian service. A second scenario would be for an energetic president to come forward and make the cause of national service his own, to argue that national service is good politics and good for the country.

The third scenario is the most problematic but also the most desirable, in that it would provide national service with its securest foundation. It would involve fostering a public sensibility to meeting societal needs in national-service terms. The public is already accustomed to thinking in such terms when it comes to military manpower needs, as is clear from the resilience of the citizen-soldier concept. To date, however, the public is less inclined to entertain such an approach with regard to civilian service (with the partial exception of conservation corps). The debate over the delivery of human services pits those who favor a market approach against those who support the expansion of government agencies to deliver such services. To break out of this typical "conservative versus liberal" mind-set means no less than a paradigmatic shift in American policy thought. Yet such a shift is essential if we are to meet the challenges that currently confront American society. A few examples should help indicate the range of problems with which national service could deal.

America is aging quickly. Americans over eighty-five years of age make up the fastest-growing segment of our population, increasing from 600,000 in 1950 to 1.5 million in 1980 to more than 4 million in 2010. Four out of ten of these "old old" people need some kind of help from another person. Already 1.4 million people live in nursing homes; as many as a third could live at home, if someone were around to help them get outside the house, to run errands, to deliver meals. Without national servers, Americans will be spending vastly greater sums to support a nationwide corporate caretaking system for the aged—a prospect that almost everyone regards with dread.

National service could help families cope with Alzheimer's disease. An incurable mental disorder that causes deterioration of the memory and reasoning abilities,

Alzheimer's afflicts some two million Americans. Its direct costs are estimated at $20 billion. The indirect costs may be even greater. The need for constant care places severe emotional burdens on relatives. Just to give family members a temporary break from caring for an Alzheimer's victim—whether through home visits or adult day-care centers—would be a major help.

In recent years, the cities of America have been inundated with the "deinstitutionalized" mentally ill. From 1965 to 1980, the number of patients in mental hospitals fell from 475,000 to 137,000, with many of those released ending up on the street. Many of these would be better off back in institutions, but current staff costs make this financially infeasible. National service, by providing low-level personnel for work in mental hospitals (much as happened in World War II with the use of conscientious objectors) would offer a way out. The alternative is to allow cities to become increasingly crowded with people incapable of taking care of themselves—and to make America increasingly callous toward the plight of the mentally ill on their doorstep.

The civic philosophy underlying national service takes a unique view of the relationship between citizen rights and duties. In 1961, John F. Kennedy, in a one-sided call for citizen duties, proclaimed, "Ask not what your country can do for you, but what you can do for your country." By the 1970s, the Democratic party had turned this admonition on its head. "Ask what your country can do for you," liberals proclaimed, "but not what you can do for your country." In the 1980s, the age of laissez-faire Republicans, the mood was: "Ask neither what your country can do for you nor what you can do for your country." National service points to a much more balanced approach to citizenship. "Ask what your country can do for you," it urges, "*and* what you can do for your country."

Religion as a Community Resource
BRYAN R. WILSON

Bryan Wilson, internationally known sociologist of religion, attended the University College of Leicester and earned a bachelor of science degree in economics with first-class honors from the University of London. His other degrees include an M.A. from Oxford University and a Ph.D. from the London School of Economics.

Since 1963, Professor Wilson has been a Fellow of All Souls College, Oxford, where he is also a reader of sociology. In addition, he has held a number of honorary appointments and consultancies, including visiting professorships in Sweden, Belgium, Canada, Australia, and Ghana. In 1985, he was named adviser to the Alister Hardy Center, a research unit on religious experience at Oxford.

Dr. Wilson is a prolific writer with eighty-three published articles, books, and lectures to his credit. His articles have appeared in such publications as *The Journal for the Scientific Study of Religion, Encounter, Sociological Analysis, Religion Today,* and the *British Journal of Sociology.* Among his books are *Religion in Sociological Perspective* (1982) and *Contemporary Transformation of Religion* (1976).

While visiting Ball State University, Professor Wilson delivered two lectures, one for the Center for Middletown Studies and the other for the Provost's Lecture Series. Both lectures are printed in full.

R ELIGION HAS OFTEN BEEN represented to us as essentially an individual concern. The whole conception of conversion, for example, from the time of St. Paul on the road to Damascus, and the revivification of this concept in the Puritan, Pietist, and Evangelical religious traditions of Protestantism has militated for an understanding of religion as primarily a matter for the individual human heart. In the modern world, where religion is largely, as sociologists say, "privatized"—a matter of personal faith rather than of social obligation—this idea of religion as a matter finally for the individual person taken in isolation has acquired added vigor. On the other hand, religion as organized in the great Christian churches—Catholic, Orthodox, Lutheran, Anglican, or Methodist—has also often been presented as a global phenomenon. The very words *catholic* and *ecumenical* indicate the claims of the churches to assume a universal competence and relevance. Some of these great churches are organized hierarchically and on a worldwide scale, with a head of affairs whose parish is the whole earth, and whose immediate subordinates take charge of particular territories or departments.

Neither of these representations of religion can be denied all validity. Religion is, especially nowadays, often a private matter, so much so that even in the United States—where public religious practice remains at the very high level (by the standard of other Christian countries) of 40 to 45 percent of the people attending church every Sunday—the vast majority of Americans, according to a Gallup survey, regard it as an inalienable right for the individual to arrive at his own beliefs, independent of all churches and synagogues. On the other hand, there is no way of denying that the Catholic Church in particular for centuries operated as if it were not only a world power but also the final arbiter of moral, political, and even economic behavior as well as the sole legitimate purveyor of spiritual truth. Yet, what I want to suggest, despite these respective individual and global manifestations, is that the natural locale of religion is neither the single person nor the large-scale society, but the community.

To make my case, I must specify my terms. By "community," I refer to the continuing company of people whose lives are conducted at a primary level, in face-to-face relationships among persons who are known as such (and not merely impersonal role-performers). Such a community is fairly well fixed in a locality, so that there is reinforcement by geographic association of the social group. Essentially, and following sociological practice, I am making a firm distinction—not always followed in everyday usage—between the society and the community. The former is a large agglomeration of people distributed over a wide expanse, most probably sharing a common language and a more or less common culture (although, in time past, both of these were often subject to considerable local variation), and integrated by common political and economic involvements. The community, in contrast, is small, cohesive, and local. In using the term *religion*, I do not confine myself to any one tradition. I do not echo the Anglican clergyman who declared that when he said "religion," he meant Christianity, and by "Christianity" he meant Christianity as purveyed by the agencies of the Church of England, and that in alluding to the Church of England, he meant quite specifically the evangelical party within that church. My prospectus is the opposite. When I say "religion," I mean the received traditions of all or any of the great faiths and indeed also many forms of practice that are not confined within any of those great traditions. I do not imply, however, that religion includes every sort of recourse to the supernatural: to be designated as religion such recourse must have a social dimension. The conception of what the supernatural is, how it operates, and how it relates to the empirical quotidian world, must be socially articulated—it cannot derive solely from private predilections, or from the fantastic, obsessive, or neurotic projections of one person.

To put into perspective the essential nature of religion, let me step out of the contemporary world and refer to a distinction forged by anthropologists and sociologists in regard to religion in tribal and traditional society—a distinction in the functions, motivations, practices, and institutions pertaining to the supernatural as a resource, on the one hand, for the community and, on the other, for the individual. The distinction is between religion and magic. This distinction is not established in theological terms; it is not normative or prescriptive, and does not in the slightest imply that religion is good and that magic is evil; rather it relies on purely formal and functional considerations. It makes plain the inherently social purposes and performances of religion in contrast to the essentially individual and private motivations of magic. Thus, religion is public activity; magic is private activity. Religion has social and public goals, whereas magic is practised for private ends. Religion seeks to reconcile men one to another: magic, in contrast, provides men with means of hostility and vengeance. Religion encourages contrition, humility, and ethical norms, whereas magic is morally neutral. Religion supplicates, celebrates, and consoles—it organizes the affective responses of social groups: magic does none of these, but seeks to constrain and to manipulate the supernatural mechanistically and instrumentally. Religion engages in a stable cultic practice to relate an articulated conception of a transcendent order to the existing social order as men know it: magic proceeds *ad hoc*, seeking specific access to elements in an inchoate and largely unknown arcane realm. Religion, then, is public spirited, whereas magic is self-interested: religion welds social groups together in unity, whereas magic drives people apart in enmity. The difference in these two approaches to the supernatural realm is that one has its origins in the known community, and the other in private self-seeking.

If it be accepted that religion is indeed a social phenomenon, let me now elaborate my contention that its basic locale is in the community rather than in the wider society. Religion functioned as a communal institution long before men became effectively organized into distinct societies as nation state or, indeed, multi-nation states. It functioned—and in Buddhism, Hinduism, and Islam functions still—without awaiting the emergence of a vast power structure, a coordinated administration, and a rationally articulated hierarchy of command, like those that came into being in the Christian tradition. The Christian Church, virtually by historical accident, inherited the mantle of empire from the Romans, and something of its hierarchic administrative structure; but this structure was not the core of religion, but only its acquired, epiphenomenal, external shell. Such an accident of history powerfully enhanced the effectiveness of Christianity, just as did its multi-ethnic constituency, its inheritance of congregational assembly from the Jewish synagogue, and its commitment to recruitment and mission—but all these things belonged to the apparatus of Christian religion, not to its essence.

Although we have grown used to identifying Christianity with the international political role that the Church performed over many centuries, all the essentials of the faith were there before the Church took settled shape or acquired wealth, territory, and a role in legitimizing the power of kings and emperors. And those essentials remain, now that, in very large measure, the Church has lost its temporal power on the international scene. Our historians have tended to write of religion in terms of the contests between popes and kings, of church and state, and of remote theological disputes among renowned scholars, and in so doing have conveyed to us a somewhat reified conception of the Church, and a rather different impression of Christianity from that which obtains at grass-root level. No doubt the power relations of church and state have an importance in the history of society, but undue preoccupation with them—as if these power struggles and elevated theological concerns were the actual substance of religion—has occluded our vision about what religion meant in the lives of ordinary people, who lived, not at the center of power, in the courts, the episcopal palaces, or the universities, but, if I may put it so, at a local level.[1] Their main preoccupations were different—the search for reassurance, the need for reconciliation among men, the desire for peace and security, and the way in which they were to cope with death, disaster, and emotional disquiet. In a sense, all of these concerns can be summarized as the demand for salvation, for cure in this life and redemption for the life hereafter; and the conception of such salvation was powerfully informed by the idea of a better life in an idealized community. For medieval Christians, death was a passage into another collective existence; and although, as John Bossy tells us,[2] the community of the dead was a model for the community of the living, in practice, the vision of that otherworldly community was of necessity a projection, in idealized form, of the community in which men lived, and which was the sole basis for their experience and their imaginings.

---

[1] Recent historians have paid more attention to the operation of religion at the local level. For example, see, for England, Keith Thomas, *Religion and the Decline of Magic: Studies in popular beliefs in sixteenth and seventeenth century England*, London: Weidenfeld and Nicolson, 1971; and, for France, Emmanuel Le Roy Ladurie, *Montaillou: Cathars and Catholics in a French Village, 1294–1324* (translated by Barbara Bray) (London: Scolar Press, 1978).

[2] John Bossy, *Christianity in the West 1400–1700* (Oxford: Oxford University Press, 1985), 31–32.

The basic commodity that religion purveys is the provision of reassurance about salvation, and it must make this provision at the point where men are, in their local communities. Whatever means are needed to attain such an end must be locally available. Thus although merit might be gained by, say, a pilgrimage, the fundamental staple of religious provision—holy communion for most mainline Christian churches—must be provided in the community. Such a basic rite is of no greater efficacy when administered by a bishop, or even by a pope, than when it is in the hands of the local priest. What needs to be done can be done and must be capable of being done locally. The priest or the minister functions for known persons, known in a community the boundaries of which are known; he does not serve anonymous masses. The relation of clergyman to people is a community relation, not an impersonal interaction of role performer and contracting customer. Indeed, to be effective, religion appears to depend upon communal contexts and to find impersonal environments fundamentally hostile. We may see the emergence of such impersonal relationships in sixteenth- and seventeenth-century Europe as a new pattern of economic organization, capitalism, began to displace the feudal and agrarian society of earlier times. Religion was displaced in the new patterns of social structure, as Max Weber perceived when he remarked:

> The typical antipathy of Catholic ethics, and following that, the Lutheran, to every capitalistic tendency, rests essentially on the repugnance of the impersonality of relations within a capitalist economy. It is the fact of impersonal relations which places certain human affairs outside the church and its influence, and prevents it from penetrating them and transforming them along ethical lines.[3]

---

[3] Max Weber, *General Economic History*, tr. F. H. Knight (New York: Collier, 1961), 262.

What Weber saw as true for those two churches at that time has become true for religion in general: impersonal contexts and structures preclude or compromise the operation of personal moral responsibility by creating patterns of interaction among role-players rather than among known persons acting on personally felt moral injunctions. As the rational and instrumental action required in the large-scale, integrated social system comes to be predominant in the whole tissue of human relations, so the personal, local, immediate concerns of community succumb to another sort of ethical ordering. Personal goodwill and individual moral sensitivity and humane considerations become irrelevant to the way the economy, the polity, and most other constellations of human relationships are conducted. Certainly, in local communities, such concerns may continue to find some place, but the world is no longer made up of innumerably replicated local communities; it is integrated on increasingly rational and pragmatic lines, so that even in local communities there is often more of a rhetoric of personal affection and moral concern than a reality; but if those elements do persist it is only in the community. The wider society is run on quite different, non-religious lines.

In many respects, as a social institution, religion stands closer to the family and kinship group than it does to the differentiated institutions of the modern large-scale society. Like the family, religion serves small groups in which each individual person is known and served as such. It transcends the individual and presents to him the conception of a sacred cosmos and an ideal community. Only in its political role, as a national or supranational church, does religion share similarities with such institutions as the polity and the economy, and its operations at that level are not part of its intrinsic and essential function. Being a communal, as distinct from a societal, institution is both the weakness and the strength of religion in the modern world. The weakness of religion lies in its remoteness from the centers of power in society, where its meaning system and its system of morality appear to be irrelevant to the purposes and understandings that inform the management of the economy, the polity, the judicature, or even the educational system. Its strength lies in the fact that even in a highly rationalized society, man is not a wholly rational being—he is not, despite the impress of modern technology, reduceable to being a mere adjunct of the machine, of the computer, or of the electronic device. He has persistent affective needs, and it becomes ever more apparent that these needs cannot be handled by the impersonal operation of societal institutions, just as they cannot be fulfilled by the individual in isolation: they must be served in a human context, in the community. Perhaps in America, the strength of religion at the communal level is more evident than anywhere else. And this is so because of the emphasis on voluntarism, on the idea—so alien in Europe, where religious obligation and, at times, religious coercion for so long prevailed—of a "choice of religion." No doubt the strength of communal religion was reinforced by the inheritance of congregational polity in the strong Puritan and Baptist traditions that so powerfully influenced religious organization in America. Perhaps because the *community* emphasis found such vigorous expression in America, religion in America has survived better than elsewhere—since it is in the community and for the community that religion fulfills its primary functions.

The communal character of religion goes back to tribal society. When Emile Durkheim sought to discover the functions of religion in simple Australian aboriginal tribes, he concluded that religion expressed the fact that men depended on a higher power than themselves—they derived their strength and acquired an awareness of their own obligations to their community by projecting onto a totem (or, as we might say, a god) the source of moral power.[4] This was a way of expressing the inexpressible, of representing the power of the group by reference to a symbolic external object that, in ways they did not realize, allowed society to assume a certain objective existence. It was a way of recognizing that, although together men and women constitute society, society also exerts constraint upon each and every one. It was a solution that grappled with the paradox that although we compose society, nonetheless, society is bigger than all of us and has a life and being of its own independent of each of us. Durkheim wrote of "society," but the groups to which he referred were only two or three hundred strong: they were primary groups of people who knew each other. The tribe was indeed not a society in the sense in which we apply that term to the United States, Britain, or the Soviet Union, which are integrated, large-scale social systems; rather, it was the equivalent of a community. Religion functioned to reinforce the sense of cohesion and consensus of that community, and so conferred on each individual a sense of identity as part of the community to which he belonged.

In the modern world, the community is manifestly less cohesive than were Durkheim's aboriginal tribes—our lives are more affected by the large-scale society, and less by the local community. Such communities are, in any case, fluid, their members mobile, their integration imperfect, and their boundaries uncertain. At many points such still recognizable communities merge into the wider society. Yet stable populations are sufficiently settled in locations of limited compass for us to say that something like community, even if attenuated, still exists. However superficially, we do know the people in our neighborhoods and share in associations and activities that are collective endeavors.

---

[4] Emile Durkheim, *Elementary Forms of the Religious Life*, tr. J. W. Swain (London: George Unwin & Allen, 1915).

The time has gone, however, when the community had sufficient cohesion and consensus to share in one religious conception and celebration of itself; and living in a community now is not enough to convey to the individual his automatic sense of identity and belonging. The constituent supports of tribal or even of medieval community have gone. Modern man no longer has real clan membership; he no longer can define himself by reference to an extended kin group. The family has withered to become a mere nuclear group—a group which, to turn a phrase, is increasingly disposed to nuclear fission—by which I allude to the growing incidence of divorce. Since the family and the kin-group are no longer stable collectivities, they can no longer give the individual a sense of identity, for identity depends on the expression of relation of one person to other persons or groups. If the family is no longer adequate to supply identity, how much less is this function served by a profession or an occupational group: no one is likely to feel that the almost adventitious circumstance of what he does as a trade is adequate to say who he is as a being.

All the other affiliations that a person may make—in unions, recreational associations, colleges or fraternities, or friendly societies—are either too segmental in their claim on allegiance, too transitory, or too much dictated by a narrow spectrum of interest to confer any encompassing identity. Such a function is approached only by the religious group. Of course, it cannot be claimed that today religious congregations provide a sense of cohesion and consensus as they did in tribal or medieval society; but virtually alone among all associations, religious bodies operate at the level not of interests but of values. They seek to command, and sometimes succeed in commanding, an encompassing allegiance, and they make that demand with the prospect of eliciting a lifetime commitment, from baptism to burial. Although modern local communities lack religious homogeneity, and churches and synagogues function in a pluralist culture where rival and sometimes competing faiths and philosophies co-exist, the religious bodies of modern societies sustain, at least in some degree, the functions of providing a sense of corporate unity that transcends mere self-interest, of conferring personal identity, and of mobilizing goodwill and moral responsibility. Above all, they cater for those affective needs of non-rational man forced to inhabit an increasingly rational and therefore increasingly desiccated wider social system.

The role of religious bodies in this respect is perhaps more emphatically evident in the United States than anywhere else in the Western world. In America, 40 to 45 percent of the people are in church on any given Sunday, compared to about 28 percent mass attenders in Belgium; about 10 to 12 percent church attenders in Britain, and somewhere in the region of 3 to 4 percent in Sweden. "Going to church" clearly has different cultural meaning and different social significance in different societies, a phenomenon that may be attributed to a variety of specific historical and social structural conditions. What the sociologist assumes, however, is that religious participation serves certain functions, and that the remarkable differences indicate that such functions are more demanded by one society than another—more demanded in the United States than, apparently, in any country of western Europe. That must be assumed unless we are prepared to write off church-going as functionless, and interpret the differences between countries as having no special meaning—and therefore, of course, as having no merit. If church-going does have functional significance, then may it not be that one or another of those ancient functions of religion, as found in earlier societies, continues to be needed even in some modern populations? It has been suggested, for example, by Will Herberg that church affiliation, Catholic or Protestant, or synagogue affiliation is one way of identifying oneself as American, that the religious congregation is in some sense a surrogate agency for the assertion and confirmation of the national identity, and that because America is a relatively new nation, forged out of migrant populations from many other societies, this need is particularly strong. That thesis could readily be associated with the more recent emphasis given to the concept of "civil religion" as a distinctly American development of commitment to a set of high ethical ideals associated with the founding of the nation and the maintenance of the democratic, civil-libertarian, and egalitarian inspiration of that foundation.

Whatever the merits of the Herberg thesis and the case for civil religion, it does appear that religion in contemporary society is an agency that provides a sense of identity for the individual, and that this function is more demanded in America than in Europe. Perhaps this need is more strongly felt precisely because the pattern of social life in America is more fluid, the population more mobile, and the experience of community life less sustained by time-honored traditions among long-settled people. Paradoxically, it may be true that where people have been longer settled and have roots in the soil, stable social structures, and marked social distinctions, where indeed there is more natural community and a long-established pattern of association, the community needs less celebration, and the individual is less uncertain about his identity, than where people are less sure about where they belong and need the reassurance of active demonstration that there really is a community to belong to.

In the search for a more rational and equitable social order, the founding fathers of the United States deliberately set aside the social patterns of European society, rejecting many elements that were intrinsic to European community life. Building up communal ties in the new nation became a much more conscious concern than it had ever been—or needed to be—in Europe. But it was a process that had to be continually renewed, since it occurred in a context of intense and rapid external change in the economy, in technology, in patterns of land settlement, in education, and in the media of communication. Given these unsettled conditions in which to attempt to build stable communities, and the phenomenal mobility of a population already more ethnically mixed than any other in the world, is it surprising that the search for identity and the quest for community should become such powerful features of American life and should have been recognized as such by sociologists?

Just how profound is such a difference from the experience of traditional societies—and, to some extent, the societies of Europe still—is not easily appreciated, but a glimpse of it may be seen in the comparison between the American experience of extensive freedom of choice in almost everything, and the almost total lack, in traditional societies, of any choice, and the lack of any imagination of what choice might mean. In the 1950s, American sociologists conducted survey research—opinion-polling—in rural Turkey. It was research that rested on bold, perhaps even miscalculated, assumptions. Turks were not then, and in considerable measure are not now, used to any extensive freedom of choice and certainly lacked the imagination that active experience of the exercise of choice conveys. Is it surprising that a very much higher proportion than would have in America answered, "Don't know," when questioned about their attitudes and preferences? One can see, in the comments on the survey made by David Riesman, how choice, even imaginary choice, was alien to their experience. Riesman wrote:

> [A] Turkish peasant . . . responding to the question as to what he would do if he were President, declared: "My God! How can you ask such a thing. How can I . . . I cannot . . . president of Turkey, master of the whole world?" Correspondingly, many of the tradition-minded in these interviews, asked

where they would like to live if they could not live in their native villages, said they would rather die: they could not conceive of living anywhere else, any more than of being somebody else.[5]

Consider the Turkish answers in terms of identity and community. These people knew who they were now, and to whom they belonged. They knew these things so well that they could not conceive of belonging to any other community. They did not need to quest for community: community was, willy-nilly, thrust upon them. Thus, it may be seen that it is where conditions for stable community are fragile that men need to create community. But creating community is not something that can be done by the application of rational planning techniques. Communities are not made: they grow. I recall the abortive gesture of some Berkeley students who, during my stay on that campus in the troubled mid-1960s, expressed their dismay at the impersonality of the university, the remoteness of their professors, and the lack of human contact with them. Some enterprising students demanded that there be set up *"a Committee to create community."* But communities do not begin with committees. Committees are rational, calculating, instrumental, and pragmatic, concerned with means, priorities, margins, and cost-efficiency: but communities are affective, indulgent, and concerned with values as ends in themselves.

It follows from all this that if there are to be agencies that sponsor, support, and sustain community life, they must be agencies that unite people, not organizations like unions or political parties, which in uniting some groups necessarily set them over against others. Merely recreational groups will not do because they command only segmentary loyalties. Even educational agencies, important

---

[5] David Riesman, "Introduction" to Daniel Lerner, *The Passing of Traditional Society: Modernizing the Middle East* (Glencoe, Ill.: Free Press, 1958), 3.

as they are—and I am unlikely in a university, and coming from a university, to wish to underestimate their importance—even educational institutions demand from most people no more than a transitory involvement. But those bodies which transcend or at least make explicit claim to transcend all mere interest groupings and which seek to command permanent commitment—namely religious bodies—are those that most effectively embody and celebrate a sense of community and in so doing confer a sense of identity.

In the mobile modern society, and especially in one of diverse social and ethnic origins, religion itself is diversified. The religious congregation is no longer the community organized for worship: it is rather only a section, and necessarily, in conformity with freedom of choice and voluntary association, a self-selection. Yet, religious bodies of quite varied origins do, in America, regularly identify with the total community, invoke the spirit of that community, and, in an increasingly ecumenical age in which concern with doctrine has markedly declined, affirm their similarities and ignore or relegate their differences. Ministers and priests seek to speak for their local communities; and, powerless as they often are in material matters, they are often regarded as keepers of the community conscience.

Just how vital religious affiliation has been to the maintenance of the community identification in America was not discovered first by Will Herberg. It was long since remarked by that perspicacious English traveller, Mrs. Frances Trollope, who wrote, not without irony, of her observations in the Midwest of the late 1820s.

> The whole people appear to be divided into an almost endless variety of religious factions; I was told in Cincinnati that to be well received in society it was indispensably necessary to declare that you belonged to some one of these factions—it did not much matter which—as far as I could make out, the Methodists were considered as the most pious,

> the Presbyterians as the most powerful, the Episcopalians and the Catholics as the most genteel, the Universalists as the most liberal, the Swedenborgians as the most musical, the Unitarians as the most enlightened, the Quakers as the most amiable, the dancing Shakers as the most amusing, and the Jews as the most interesting. Besides these there are dozens more of fancy religions whose designations I cannot remember, but declaring yourself to belong to any one of them as far as I could learn was sufficient to constitute you a respectable member of society.[6]

Not only did religious affiliation ensure your acceptability in the community, but, in those days, to infringe the moral or conventional code even in minor matters was to risk loss of church membership and, with it, loss at least of status, and perhaps of all reputation, in the community. Mrs. Trollope continued:

> Having thus far declared yourself, your next submission must be that of unqualified obedience to the will and pleasure of your elected pastor, or you will run a great risk of being "passed out of the church." This was a phrase that I perpetually heard . . . a sort of excommunication which infallibly betides those who venture . . . anything that their pastor . . . disapproves. I once heard a lady say, "I must not wear high bows on my bonnet, or I shall be passed out of our church," and another, "I must not go to see the dancing at the theatre or I shall be passed out of our church," and another, "I must not confess that I visit Mrs. J. or I shall be passed out of our church, for they say she does not belong to any church in town."[7]

Religious affiliation, then, was, if Mrs. Trollope was correct, the *sine qua non* of identification with the commu-

---

[6] Frances Trollope, *Domestic Manners of the Americans* (London: The Folio Society, 1974), 91n.
[7] *Ibid.*, 91–92n.

nity and with the agencies that provided mutual support and welfare.

In the early days after mass migration to America, religious congregations became the means of perpetuating national, ethnic, and cultural identity for particular groups. Shared religion solemnized and sacralized group custom and conventions, and even quite secular features of early European folk cultures, language not least among them, were preserved in religious contexts.[8] As America ceased to depend to the earlier extent on immigration, and as heterogeneity of its population somewhat diminished with successive generations, the earlier association of specific denominations and particular ethnic and cultural constituencies diminished. Religion became effectively a matter of choice rather than an expression of ethnic origin or inherited commitment, until today, as we have seen, religious belonging is the residual basis for a claim to identity with the community. That the old community orientation remains and may yet be awakened is evident from the occasional instances in which group identity is vigorously asserted in a religious medium. Thus, the Puerto Rican immigrants who flowed into New York and other Eastern seaboard cities in the late 1940s and 1950s felt a desperate need to assert and retain their community identity in the face of a largely alien social experience. They found the churches of their own Roman Catholic faith too indigenized and institutionalized adequately to accommodate them. As a deprived and linguistically disadvantaged minority, they simply did not "feel at home" in those churches, and in large numbers they came to express their need for a transcendent legitimation of their community identity in a different religious expression—they were readily converted by various Pentecostal sects, the intimacy, immediacy, and

---

[8] For an illustration of this point, see Nicholas Tavuchis, *Pastors and Immigrants: The Role of a Religious Elite in the Absorption of Norwegian Immigrants* (The Hague: Martinus Nijhoff, 1963).

spontaneity of whose worship spoke more directly to their needs.[9]

Such strong assertions of the communal bonding of religion are today rare in the Western world, and the reason appears to be that the social conditions for community are so much less congenial. People still seek to belong to encompassing communities, but they also often seek the freedom to escape from them. For those who have experienced the freedom of the metropolitan society, local affective bonds can appear restrictive as well as supportive. "How," as a war-time American song once asked, "you gonna keep 'em down on the farm, Now that they've seen Paree?" The "Paree" of the song represents only the superficial attractive temptations of anonymous urban life, but there are more structural forces at work in undermining communal loyalties than merely the impersonal "good time" amusements of the entertainment industry. Processes operate in today's society that derogate the local community. The imperatives of modern economy, rational planning, and systematic large-scale, often international organization, spring from sources that are indifferent to, if not hostile toward, local concerns. The wider society becomes increasingly intrusive into the life of local communities. Contemporary technology facilitates the integration of ever larger agglomerations of people in enterprises and activities that can be conceived only at the level of the total social system. To give but one example, commuting has become normal in society, and its effect on the local community is direct and dramatic—people now very rarely work and learn in the place where they sleep. The community is torn apart: as David Martin has said, "The equation of church-place-community is dislocated."[10]

---

[9] An account is provided in Roberto Poblete and Thomas O'Dea, "Anomie and the 'Quest for Community': The Formation of Sects Among the Puerto Ricans of New York," *American Catholic Sociological Review*, XXI, 1 (1960), 18–36.

[10] David Martin, "Revived Dogma and New Cult," *Daedalus*, III, 1 (1982), 55.

Instead of community, modern society offers us communication—and communication, as I need remind no one, is now often called the communications industry, a phrase which ought to represent to us a contradiction in terms. What once had as its very essence the fact of personal immediacy, trust, intimacy, and human regard of one person for a known other is now an impersonal vehicle presenting unknown, virtually anonymous persons—indeed, in the sense of fictional or stage-managed images, often unreal persons to even less known mass audiences. There is no real affective involvement, except at times the sentimental, spurious, and manipulated imitative recapitulations of it—as when the public, or a section of it, "falls in love" with one or another character in a soap opera.

Today even religion, which almost more than any other communicative activity needs the interface of real people with mutual trust, has, with the televangelists, come to adopt the impersonal imitation of genuine communication and genuine communion. Perhaps—who knows?—if the recently fallen televangelic idols had lived with real people in real communities, rather than with the communications industry, their fall would have been gentler, and there would have been gentler people to cushion its impact.

Religion was at home in the local community, and that was its strength and support, but the modern world erodes the boundaries of those easy and natural local associations. Religion remains, especially here in America, a community resource, but the question we must ask is whether, given the development of our societies, the community will be able to reassert itself to use religion as effectively as once it might have done.

American Influences on the Development of Religion

BRYAN R. WILSON

ALTHOUGH IT IS COMMONLY SUPPOSED that religion immutably transcends the accidence of time and space, and has a character of timeless and unalterable truth, the sociological evidence suggests that in being transferred from one cultural context to another, religion always undergoes significant change. In adapting to the New World over three or four centuries, Christianity necessarily changed not only in style, mood, and internal diversity, but also in its organization, in the place it acquired in society, in its social role, and, in some part, even in its acknowledged purposes. Just as contemporary Christianity will change substantially as it assimilates to other cultures, in the Third World in which it is so rapidly spreading, so, perhaps with less general awareness of the fact, did Christianity experience considerable transformation in adapting to the new and rapidly evolving culture of the New World.

The settling of America was inherently an unsettling of the preconceptions, unexamined assumptions, and social mores of the peoples who migrated to that continent, and who subsequently migrated within that continent. The settlers and later generations of Americans had to discover, much more self-consciously than was ever necessary or even possible in the Old World, the forms and norms of civil society. It was here that ancient shibboleths, received wisdom, entrenched conventions, sacred taboos, sanctified assumptions of differences in social status, and ancient legitimations of social inequality were all to be challenged.

They were challenged not solely nor even mainly in deliberate revolution, but because the exigencies of everyday life in a new environment demanded it. In the weaving of a social fabric from the diverse strands that had to be included in the pattern, the new society—American society—began with the apparent disadvantage of lacking that inheritance common to older societies of a cohesive religious tradition. Indeed, as a refuge for persecuted religious minorities, America was from the outset a country that almost deliberately encouraged religious diversity.

Whereas in Europe, religious dissent or deviation was regarded as a threat to social cohesion, in America diversity in religion was in itself a social reality long before the formal framework of the wider, that is to say, federal, society was established. Whereas, in Europe, the Church had long been used to legitimize the monarch, in America, the state was instituted with only the barest of references to religious belief. Whereas in Europe, religious observance had long been a matter of obligation for the subjects of the state, in America, the voluntaristic principle was a concomitant of religious pluralism. The significance of these differences is evident when it is recalled that the Christian Church in general, and each separate ancient branch of it, had claimed an exclusive monopoly of the complete truth. In Europe, those who rejected the ministrations of that branch of the Church that was established in their society (whether Catholic, Lutheran, Reformed, or Anglican) were necessarily regarded as "nonconformists" or "dissenters," if not as outright heretics or even miscreants. In America, the claims to exclusivity of truth were necessarily tempered and eventually entirely eroded simply because of the plural religious traditions—initially almost exclusively Christian traditions—to which American society was from the outset committed.

In the Old World, in each separate state religious uniformity was seen as an indispensable condition for social cohesion. But from the earliest days, America had to function without the prop of religious obligation that had supported state and civil society in Europe. Indeed, rather than religious uniformity, diversity and tolerance became the preconditions in terms of which American society was to be held together. The old alliance of social institutions that prevailed in European societies maintained the close hegemony of monarch and prelate. There, the temporal power of the state was legitimized by the spiritual power of the church, and the legal status of the church was underwritten by the coercive force monopolized by the state. In America, of necessity new patterns evolved and different institutions came into association. Alexis de Tocqueville found remarkable the easy co-existence of religion and democracy.[1] These were strange bedfellows in the eyes of a European aristocrat accustomed to religion that was itself hierarchic and that was explicitly committed to the support of hierarchy in both the social and spiritual domains. In his country democratic and revolutionary tendencies had been and continued to be associated with anticlericalism. In America, the boundaries of church and state were drawn with very different assumptions in mind.

The potential divisiveness of religious pluralism was transcended in America by an ethic which, implicitly, claimed superiority to all religious positions: namely, the commitment to tolerance and the liberty of conscience. The new state, the federation of American states, based its

---

[1] Tocqueville commented, "America is the most democratic country in the world, and it is at the same time . . . the country in which the Roman Catholic religion makes most progress. At first sight this is surprising. . . . Equality inclines men to wish to form their own opinions; but, on the other hand, it imbues them with the taste and the idea of unity, simplicity, and impartiality in the power which governs society. Men living in democratic times are therefore very prone to shake off all religious authority; but if they consent to subject themselves to any authority of this kind, they choose at least it should be single and uniform." *Democracy in America*, ed. Richard D. Heffner (New York: The New American Library, 1956), 155–56.

conception of cohesion on toleration rather than on commitment to uniform religious belief and practice. In this sense, the American vision of society manifestly surpassed in its ethical standards anything that had been seen in countries committed to exclusivistic religious creeds and to organizations in which those creeds were enshrined. There is, however, another aspect of tolerance, which is its inherent tendency to cultivate a relativistic appraisal of all religious positions. In America, no religion can claim superiority in the social or civic sense: all religions are of equal standing, and since they are equal, it would demand a certain hauteur almost tantamount to hubris for any denomination too strenuously to demand special rights by virtue of a claim to exclusive or even superior access to ultimate truth. In the context of liberal tolerance, a religious movement that makes such claims relegates itself to the status of a sect. The truth-claims of any denomination that wishes to be recognized as part of mainstream religion are thus necessarily subordinated to the demand that tolerance be shown toward all.

Today, relativism not only characterizes the general religious ethos of America, but even penetrates the bastions of fundamentalism. Let me remind you of Jerry Falwell's response to a dictum of Bailey Smith, president of the Southern Baptist Convention—a dictum that just a few decades ago would have been entirely acceptable to the vast majority of Christians of any persuasion. Bailey Smith is reported to have said, "At great political rallies . . . you have a Protestant to pray, a Catholic to pray, and then you have a Jew to pray. With all due respect to those dear people, my friends, God Almighty does not hear the prayer of a Jew." This sentiment is today unacceptable to liberal Christians and led even an evangelical like Mr. Falwell to contradict it in highly relativist terms. What he said was,

This is a time for Catholics, Protestants, Jews, Mormons, and all Americans to rise above every effort to polarize us in our efforts to return this nation to the commitment to the moral principles on which America was built. America is a pluralist republic. We cannot survive if we allow it to become anything else. God hears the cry of any sincere person who calls on him.[2]

Thus pluralism promotes tolerance; tolerance fosters relativism; and the quality of sincerity becomes more important than what it is that one is sincere about. The fact of believing—at least within certain, but perhaps expanding, limits—comes to transcend in importance the substance of things believed. Much as believers committed to one tradition may regret the demise of unifying belief, in an unalterably pluralistic world tolerance and liberty of conscience inevitably command ethical precedence.

---

[2] These statements are quoted in Robert T. Handy, *A Christian America: Protestant Hopes and Historical Realities* (New York: Oxford University Press, 2nd ed., 1984), 205. That the judgments of the Supreme Court have been leading in the same direction is illustrated in comments made on the extension of the right of exemption from compulsory military service to those who do not belong to religious groups but who hold ethical convictions that constitute conscientious objection: "The Supreme Court's implicit definition of religion, based on *Seeger* and *Welsh*, has become both more formalized and more individualized: that is, an individual's religion is defined not by the content of his/her beliefs, but by the formal place those beliefs hold in the conscience. Similarly, religion is considered an individual phenomenon, irrespective of any organizational or institutional commitments." N.J. Demerath II and Rhys H. Williams, "A Mythical Past and Uncertain Future" in Thomas Robbins and Roland Robertson, eds., *Church-State Relations: Tensions and Transitions* (New Brunswick: Transaction Books, 1987), 80. Public opinion confirms the trend: "A 1978 Gallup poll found that 80 per cent of Americans agreed that 'an individual should arrive at his own religious beliefs independent of any churches or synagogues.'" Robert Bellah et al., *Habits of the Heart* (Berkeley and Los Angeles: University of California Press, 1985), 228. The implication of these judgments and opinions is that individual conscience and personal sincerity are the real criteria of worth, a position that admits of complete relativism with respect to the content and provenience of beliefs, and the warranty for them.

Given religious pluralism in a highly diversified society, the state becomes the authority that presides, neutrally but transcendently, over the various religious denominations. The state determines the boundaries within which religious bodies may operate, and to do this the state must be deliberately and self-consciously secular, assuming the role of a superior moral agency. This secularization of the state, as it occurred in America, did not imply the erosion of popular religion—far from it—but it did powerfully influence the secularization of the social system extruding religious concerns and supernatural assumptions from the major institutions of social life—following the polity and the judicature, the economy, public education, and public health care. Paradoxically, it is the elimination of religious influence from the operation of the state and from public institutions that guarantees the freedom of religion. Such a secular state was first created in America.

Today, in the Western world, the merits of toleration need no special advocacy: they are taken for granted. In one country after another, albeit in some of them only since the end of the second World War, the basic rights of free association and the freedom of belief and the right to teach one's beliefs or to change them have been affirmed, and these freedoms are enshrined in the resolutions of the United Nations and the Council of Europe. But such freedom might not have come, and would certainly not have come so quickly, but for the unique circumstances of the United States and the early imperative to shift the basis of social cohesion from uniformity of belief to a common tolerance for diverse beliefs. There is one further implication. The toleration of diverse religious groups rests on the democratic assumption that men have equal rights to liberty of conscience. This freedom went further than mere toleration of different religious ideas and of the groups that espoused them. The basic principle is at once more radical and more far-reaching than that of guaranteeing the rights of already existing groups. Implicitly, it accords individual freedom of conscience to follow any religion *or none*. It admits the principle of tolerance for religions as yet unknown. Thus, it is more radical than the toleration acts that were first instituted in England just three hundred years ago, in 1688, which accorded a measure of closely circumscribed toleration, but only to certain restricted variations of Christian and, even more particularly, of Protestant belief. In making liberty of conscience the criterion, religious toleration in the United States acclaimed a conception of individual human rights far broader and more basic than mere rights to religious freedom.

The consequences of the creation of the secular state were not confined to matters of religious freedom: there were consequences also for the way in which Christianity was in the future to be organized not only in America, but eventually everywhere that Christian pluralism existed. Older conceptions of religious diversity, drawn from the European context, assumed an inherent superiority-inferiority relation between different versions of the faith. A church that was established legally by the state, as were the Lutheran Church in Sweden and the Anglican Church in England, or a church that was officially recognized—the Catholic Church in France, Austria, Italy, and Spain—was regarded and regarded itself as a superior religion. Dissenting groups that separated from the dominant church—where such dissent was permitted at all—were generally seen, both by public officials and by the general public, as necessarily inferior—the religions of inferior, deviant, and perhaps disruptive people. Thus, even when there was toleration—and it occurred in Protestant lands in greater measure than in Catholic countries—the dissident bodies were stigmatized: they were derogated as "sects." Clearly, in anathematizing separatists, the Church perpetuated these evaluative judgments, and the categories of "church" and "sect" passed into European sociological literature as the two basic types of Christian organization.[3]

The development of Christianity in America, however, necessarily brought such a categorization into question, at first in America and subsequently elsewhere in Christendom. In America, there was no established or officially approved religion: in the European sense, there really was no Church, written with a capital "C." Similarly, since all men were to be regarded as equal before the law, so, too, were their religions—it might be said that in the derogatory sense of the term as it was deployed in Europe there were, in America, no sects. In Europe, church and sect had been seen as dichotomous principles of religious organization, and even as divergent and dialectically opposed strands within Christian history. In America, there were denominations, and with respect to their official status, all religious bodies—regardless of their internal structure, their ideological commitment, their claims to legitimacy, or the social status of their votaries—were to be seen as simply differing denominational persuasions, each of which should be accorded full religious dignity. That term *denomination* has in itself a certain studied neutrality that disavows the encompassing claims of a body that styles itself "the Church," and avoids the pejorative connotations usually intended when a movement is called "a sect."

Since the claims of a church were diminished, and those of a sect enhanced in this new organizational conception of Christianity, it is not surprising that H. Richard Niebuhr, in reviewing religion in early twentieth-century America, could propound the dictum that a sect could persist for only one generation—that with the coming of the second generation the sect became denominational-

---

[3] The sociological *locus classicus* that established the concepts of sect and church is Ernst Troeltsch, *The Social Teaching of the Christian Churches*, tr. O. Wyon (New York: Macmillan, 1931).

ized, acquiring social respectability and taking its place as an equal among other religious bodies.[4] If Niebuhr was not entirely right—for some sects do persist as such over several generations[5]—nonetheless, the tendency for all religious bodies to acquire similarity of status, despite their historically widely divergent claims, was one that was conspicuous in the United States.

What, then, had occurred in the development of Christianity in America was that religion had become a matter of voluntary adherence, and the religious body had become a voluntary association. That was a feature of Christianity that had disappeared after the time of Constantine. Since the early days of persecution, Christianity had itself become a matter of obligation—obligation not infrequently reinforced by coercive measures approved by the Church and implemented by the state. In America, Christianity, in losing its official status, became dependent upon the goodwill and voluntary commitment of the people. The effect of such voluntarism, contrary to what European governments and established churchmen might have supposed, was not the diminution of religious practice and belief, but rather the contrary. Subscription to religion became more vigorous once voluntarism became the accepted principle, not less, as the supporters of coercive obligation appear to have assumed. Church attendance and church membership have remained higher in the United States than in all but two or three European countries. Voluntary religious bodies remain stronger in the United States than the once-compulsory state churches of such countries as Sweden, England, and Scotland.

The presumptive equality of status of different religious bodies has also helped to facilitate conversations of

---

[4] The thesis is propounded in H. Richard Niebuhr, *Social Sources of Denominationalism* (New York: Holt, 1929).

[5] For a refutation of the Niebuhr thesis, see B. R. Wilson, "An Analysis of Sect Development," *American Sociological Review*, 24, 1 (1959), 3–15.

rapprochement among them. Although other influences have also affected the ecumenical movement, particularly the gradual erosion of doctrinal differences that have been inherited from the past and that arose in circumstances very different from those prevailing in recent times, the parity of status of denominations has done much to make ecumenical dialogue easier. The exaggerated claims of traditional European churches that were supported by the state have been deflated, and this has made mutual respect and acceptability among Christians of different persuasions and origins a more readily accomplished and perhaps a more ardently desired goal.

Although America became the home of numerous religious refugees, it drew, from quite early times, many who claimed no particular religious heritage. A new mass public came into being who were there to be recruited. These were not the subservient classes of Europe, many of whom were lapsed or Laodicean in their religious commitment, but who could, nonetheless, be treated still as nominal members of the dominant church. Rather, these Americans were a new type of public, a people increasingly aware of their freedom of choice and at the same time available for the proselytizing efforts of the churches. It is no accident that the revivalist tradition, and particularly that of the open-air or tent revival campaign, should be so predominantly an American mode of religious enterprise. Of course, Christians had long expected conversion of outsiders, but for centuries in Europe, conversion had been a peripheral and individual phenomenon. For the mainline churches it was virtually irrelevant or even suspect, and it prevailed only in the newly emerging experientially oriented sects such as Moravians and Methodists. But in the United States the mass exposure of large publics to religious propaganda and exhortatory and emotional preaching became a dominant religious style,[6] and it is a style that,

---

[6] Perry Miller, *The Life of the Mind in America* (London; Gollancz,

in the transmuted form of televangelism, continues in America to this day.

Early revivalism was, of course, regarded as a consequence of the spontaneous operation of the Holy Spirit. That Spirit had only very rarely intruded upon the settled, ordered, and traditionalized life of the churches in the Old World; but once Europeans had become acquainted with revivalism in America, the expectation of similar experiences in Europe was not long in coming to fulfillment. The

---

1966), 13, writes of revival, "In early nineteenth century America it was accepted as a unique American ritual," and in the same passage he quotes Robert Baird (*Religion in America*, 1844), as saying of the diverse attitudes to revivals in Europe and America, "Christians on one side of the Atlantic expect them and on the other they do not." Despite the operation of Wesley and Whitefield in their eighteenth-century field-preaching, which Miller notes, the British still considered revivalism as uniquely American, at least until the impact of Finney. Mrs. Frances Trollope, visiting America at virtually the same time as Tocqueville, wrote: "We had not been many months in Cincinnati when our curiosity was excited by hearing the 'revival' talked of by every one we met . . . 'The revival will be very full'—'We shall be constantly engaged during the revival'—were the phrases we constantly heard repeated, and for a long time, without in the least comprehending what was meant; but at length I learnt that the un-national church of America required to be roused, at regular intervals, to greater energy and exertion." Frances Trollope, *Domestic Manners of the Americans*, ed. Herbert van Thal (London: The Folio Society, 1974), 71 (first published 1832). In a subsequent footnote, Mrs. Trollope responded to critics who apprised her of the fact that revivals also occurred by this time in England. She scarcely believed it at first, saying that reivals, "if existing at all, could only be met with among persons in a much lower station in life than any I have quoted as specimens in America." But even this opinion had to be revised as she was obliged to acknowledge that "fearful profanation of the holy name of religion" had "rapidly increased," and that the "national church" in England and the "guardian protection which its episcopal authority" seemed "to promise against its desecration by the ever-varying innovations of sectarian licence" was a protection no longer (*Ibid.*, 72). Later, Mrs. Trollope saw worse horrors, at a camp meeting in Indiana in 1829, for that, too, was a totally unfamiliar manifestation of religiosity which she, however, could not admit to be such, for she recorded that "at length, the atrocious wickedness of this horrible scene increased to a degree of grossness, that drove us from our station" (*Ibid.*, 135).

preaching of Whitefield and Wesley was powerfully influenced by the revival experience in America, and a new style of religion was introduced to the working classes of England and Wales. If it fell short of the intensity which American revivalism usually manifested, that may be attributed to the difference of cultural contexts and to the strength of the established church and of those who, sometimes for more than merely religious reasons, found it politic to support that church.[7] But the import-export balance of spiritual trade was shifting: the New World was ceasing to be dependent for its modes of religious expression and organization on the Old, and American revivalists were increasingly disposed, in the early decades of the nineteenth century, to undertake preaching missions to Britain.

Although revivalism itself was a uniquely transatlantic product, introducing more informality and demotic spontaneity into religion, there was a yet more characteristically American development to follow. The United States was, of necessity, a more rationally planned and deliberatively constituted society than any in Europe (not even excepting Napoleonic France). America was an explicitly self-consciously organized social system. Since the polity, the judicature, and social administration were so much the product of rational organization, it is not surprising that similar influences became apparent in religion generally, even in revivalism; for whereas the staid religious forms of the mainline churches drew on European tradition, revivalism, as a peculiarly American phenomenon, was susceptible to secular influences that were distinctly American. Thus, whereas for Jonathan Edwards in the 1730s men could wait for the Holy Spirit to move them individually, a century later, for Charles Finney, there was no reason why revivals should not be planned and organized, and this for a mass public.[8] If the final work of revival was still to be a

---

[7] P. Miller, *op. cit.*, comments on the contrast, 13.

[8] For an account of Finney's approach to revivals, see William G. McLoughlin, Jr., *Modern Revivalism* (New York: Ronald Press, 1959).

mystery of God, men could at least make a deliberate and systematic preparation for it. In some respects, the revival campaign exhibits in paradoxical juxtaposition two contrasting facets of the American religious genius: on the one hand, openness to experience and the spontaneity of individual expression, and on the other, the commitment to the rationally planned organization and systematic procedures by which American society itself was shaped. Both currents persist in contemporary Christianity, of course, but that they do so may be largely attributed to the development of religion in America.

The revivalistic strain in Christianity has never disappeared, different as the techniques of campaigning and the media of outreach in an electronic age have become. Campaigns, less local, less dependent on geography, have been extended to whole regions or nations. The revivalists themselves have run the risk of becoming media stars—a risk they have not always resisted—and this trend reflects the impact on religious ministry of the secular culture. Nor has the influence of that culture been confined to techniques of evangelism: in celebrated cases, with the adoption of its technical facilities, the values of secular culture have been swallowed too.

The revivalist tradition has left its mark on other changing patterns of Christian faith and practice, and these too have had their origin in the United States. The Holiness movements of the late nineteenth century and the emergence of modern Pentecostalism, the origins of which may be precisely located in Topeka, Kansas, in 1900, manifest evident continuities with revival religion.[9] Pentecostalism is ecstatic Christianity. It takes its name from the doctrine of gifts of the Spirit as defined in I Corinthians, and espe-

---

[9] For a history of the Holiness movement, see Timothy L. Smith, *Called Unto Holiness: The Story of the Nazarenes* (Kansas City: Nazarene Pub. House, 1963). For the early development of Pentecostalism, see Robert Mapes Anderson, *Vision of the Disinherited: The Making of American Pentecostalism* (New York: Oxford University Press, 1979).

cially the gift of speaking in unknown tongues that was manifested to the apostles at Pentecost. The ecstasy has been tempered, but in essence the *raison d'être* of Pentecostalism is to assert the validity of Holy Ghost inspiration. It is religion in which spontaneity, immediacy, informality, and individual experience are at a premium, and if it arose initially among the disinherited populations of American cities, it found an echo in similar social strata throughout Christendom. Its lines of influence have been well traced, and the history of Pentecostalism shows how this American form of Christianity spread to Sweden and then to England, Holland, Germany, and throughout especially Protestant Europe and Russia in the first two or three decades of the century, and how, after World War II, Pentecostalism made dramatic inroads into Catholic countries, from Italy to Chile, and from Portugal to Brazil.[10]

Pentecostalism has been seen as a religion of the oppressed, and it was for a time easy to identify its evident emotionalism and its emphasis on literal biblicism with anti-intellectualism and that compensatory form of Christianity so attractive to the socially deprived. But, beginning in 1958, in an Episcopal church in Van Nuys, California, another inspirational movement began, emphasizing the same charismata, and quickly sweeping through the congregations of mainline churches in the following two decades.[11] Since the votaries of this Charismatic Renewal movement were self-evidently not disinherited—at least not economically—but were comfortable middle-class citi-

---

[10] On the worldwide spread of Pentecostalism, see Nils Block-Hoell, *The Pentecostal Movement* (London: Allen & Unwin, 1964); Walter J. Hollenweger, *The Pentecostals* (London: SCM Press, 1972); for an example of the spread of Pentecostalism in Latin America, see C. Lalive d'Epinay, *Haven of the Masses* (London: Lutterworth Press, 1969).

[11] See, on charismatic renewal, Richard Quebedeaux, *The New Charismatics* (New York: Doubleday, 1976); on the gifts of the Spirit as such, see Cyril G. Williams, *Tongues of the Spirit* (Cardiff: University of Wales Press), 1981.

zens, new theories were needed to explain the appeal to them of ecstatic religious experience. If they were seeking compensation it was for deprivation that was not specifically economic.[12] If Christianity's appeal is in part to be expressed in the words "Come unto me, all ye that labor and are heavy laden," as Scripture puts it, then the burdens for the devotees of Charismatic Renewal were perhaps of social and psychological rather than of material impoverishment. Whatever the explanation, Charismatic Renewal spread even more rapidly than the earlier Pentecostalism. It spread not as a movement spawning a congeries of new sects, but as a cult within the traditional churches both Protestant and Catholic; and the authorities of those churches—much as they had condemned earlier Pentecostalism as schismatic and perhaps as heretical—to this new phenomenon appeared unable or unwilling to say nay. A new wave of originally and perhaps characteristically American spirituality broke across the world, changing the face of Christendom, and this despite the implicit destructuring tendencies with which inspirationalist movements always confront the received order of the traditional churches.

The diversity among the currents of American religious thought, practice, and organization can scarcely be encompassed in one lecture, and I have selected those tendencies that have had an influence on the structure and culture of Christianity worldwide. Inevitably, those currents have been innovatory rather than conservative (conservative in the sense of preserving and reinforcing tradition). Innovation was, and perhaps still is, to be expected from a new nation organized in a new way and in a new natural environment, and it is understandable that, although such innovation affects traditional mainline religion, its extreme forms are most pronounced in sectarian

---

[12] The concept of relative deprivation is discussed in Charles Y. Glock and Rodney Stark, *Religion and Society in Tension* (Chicago: Rand McNally, 1965), 242–59.

expression. This phenomenon becomes apparent in the divergent moods that have been evident in those Christian movements that are indigenous to America: moods of serene, if not triumphalist, worldly optimism, and of its opposite, the despair of any future for the world order under the present dispensation.[13]

America as a land of promise, and Americans as a nation in receipt of special divine favor are themes that occur in multitudinous forms, from the Social Gospel at the turn of the last century to the Mormon claims that the American continent has a special divine history and a special divine destiny. Even literal biblicists embraced a similar optimism in their expectation of the steady improvement of the age and the triumph of mission that were to usher in the millennium on earth (with the Second Advent to follow). If that specific calendar was less often consulted once war and depression occurred, other more individualistic species of optimistic faith persisted in America and were diffused elsewhere. A spate of inspirationalist literature that reached its zenith perhaps in the 1930s preached a gospel popularly called "the power of positive thinking," and that current of spirituality was expressed even more emphatically in Christian Science and the various New Thought movements.[14] The emphasis is wholly American: man as a reflection of God, made in his image and likeness; religion as a mental therapy; the world as one's oyster to

---

[13] These two moods are, of course, analogues of the divergent tendencies noted in a psychological mode as "healthy-minded" and "twice-born" dispositions to religion by William James, *The Varieties of Religious Experience* (New York: Collier Books, 1961) (originally published in 1902).

[14] On this, see Louis Schneider and Sanford M. Dornbusch, *Popular Religion: Inspirational Books in America* (Chicago: Chicago University Press, 1958). On Christian Science, Charles S. Braden, *Christian Science Today* (Dallas: Southern Methodist University Press, 1958) is still useful, and on New Thought, Charles S. Braden, *Spirits in Rebellion: The Rise and Development of New Thought* (Dallas: Southern Methodist University Press, 1963) remains the best account.

be prized open and to yield up its pearl. Here was a Christianity in sharp contrast to the traditional emphasis on man's burden of sin; the world as a vale of tears, a severe trial to be meritoriously endured in this life if one were to inherit the next. The optimism, born perhaps of an expanding society, a moving westward frontier, a burgeoning economy, and a future as the world's greatest power, penetrated Christianity, both Catholic and Protestant, and even contemporary Judaism. In the face of such a social experience, man as the miserable sinner, God as the inscrutable judge, gave way to a Christianity more of the son than of the father, more of love than of justice. A justified hedonism replaced the ascetic precepts of the past, and even evangelical religion, which once emphasized a severe moral code, came, among televangelists like Jim and Tammy Bakker, to legitimize consumerism and luxury rather than the spirituality and frugality emphasized in the Protestant past.[15]

Yet, even in a land of promise, some promises, and promises to some, remain unredeemed. An excess of promise and a dearth of fulfillment promote despair, and that other Christian theme, which depicts man's sojourn in the world as a catalogue of woe to be borne until divine intervention occurs, has also found more vigorous, more persistent, and more systematic expression in America than ever it did in the intermittent outbursts of millenarianism in the Old World. Whereas in Europe, those despairing of the world gave brief life to spasmodic movements or to segregated congregations minuscule in size and without social influence, in America the dream of the premillennial ad-

---

[15] James Davison Hunter, *American Evangelicalism: Conservative Religion and the Quandary of Modernity* (New Brunswick: Rutgers University Press, 1983), 87–91, enlarges on the ways in which evangelical religion has been softened and polished in what he calls a modified accommodation to the cultural plurality of modernity. Very similar observations are made by Wade Clark Roof, "The Study of Social Change in Religion," in Phillip E. Hammond, ed., *The Sacred in a Secular Age* (Berkeley and Los Angeles: University of California Press, 1985), 160.

vent, following a devastating Armageddon, gave rise to well-organized mass movements which have endured for well over a century, which have grown, and which disseminate their vision world-wide. Although the most conspicuous representative of this current is the Watchtower Society of Jehovah's Witnesses, it remains a dominant theme for Seventh-day Adventists and the Worldwide Church of God, in the numerous Pentecostal movements, and among some other evangelical groups. All these bodies are of American provenience,[16] and they constitute the biggest sects in Christendom worldwide.

Pluralism and tolerance, denominational organization, revivalism, expressive religion, Christian optimism, and Christian pessimism—these are all influences that in shaping American Christianity have also shaped Christianity throughout the world. Religion is not, as some believers sometimes like to suppose, a timeless and changeless constellation of beliefs, values, practices, attitudes, and institutions. It is a responsive and at times even volatile agency through which human hopes and fears are expressed, and which picks up the values and procedures, the structures and the techniques prevalent in the wider society. In America, Western man embarked on a new venture in living together that entailed new practices, new needs, and new responses. Religion—specifically Christianity—did much to shape the pattern of American life, but it has in turn drawn extensively from that society, and what it has acquired it has in large part passed on to religion in the wider world.

---

[16] On Jehovah's Witnesses, see James A. Beckford, *The Trumpet of Prophecy* (Oxford: Blackwell, 1976); and M. James Penton, *Apocalypse Delayed* (Toronto: University of Toronto Press, 1985). Perhaps the most useful general conspectus of Seventh-day Adventism is that by Malcolm Bull and Keith Lockhart, *The Quiet American* (New York: Harper and Row), forthcoming 1989.

The Premise of the U.S. Constitutional System

PAUL SARBANES

The Honorable Paul S. Sarbanes has represented the state of Maryland in the United States Senate since 1976. He is chair of the Joint Economic Committee and a member of the Senate Foreign Relations Committee, where he chairs the subcommittee on Near Eastern and South Asian Affairs. He also presides over the subcommittee on International Finance and Monetary Policy, which reports to the Senate Committee on Secret Military Assistance to Iran and the Nicaraguan Opposition.

Before his election to the Senate, Sarbanes was a three-term member of the United States House of Representatives. There he served as a junior member of the select drafting committee that honed the articles of impeachment during the proceedings against Richard Nixon.

Senator Sarbanes earned his undergraduate degree from Princeton University, and he attended Oxford University as a Rhodes Scholar. After graduation from Harvard Law School, he practiced law with two Baltimore firms and served in the Maryland House of Delegates.

Senator Sarbanes's presentation at Ball State University was designated the fourteenth Stephen J. and Beatrice Brademas Lecture. This annual lecture is named for the parents of former U.S. Representative John Brademas of Indiana, now president of New York University.

THE MEN WHO MET in Philadelphia to decide how this country should be governed had been educated thoroughly in the classical tradition and in the political theory of the Greeks and the Romans.

Henry Steele Commager, speaking of the delegates to the Constitutional Convention, reminds us that all of them knew Plutarch and Thucydides and Tacitus and were familiar with the doctrines of civil liberty as taught by such men as Plato, Demosthenes, and Cicero. Commager goes on to speak of the "continuous rain of references to the experience of the ancient world in the debates in the Federal Convention . . . and the preoccupation with ancient history . . . in the Federalist Papers." For those of us who decry the low estate into which the discipline of history has fallen in our schools and universities, it is perhaps sobering to reflect with Commager that the men who fought the revolution and wrote the federal and state constitutions and the bills of rights were brought up on the histories of Greece and Rome and England.

Catherine Drinker Bowen, in her splendid book *Miracle at Philadelphia*, records that

> there was a notion in Europe that Americans were proceeding in their government upon Greek principles. President Willard of Harvard in 1788 received a letter from an English sympathiser, saying that the writer had heard there was to be a revival of the Olympic games in America. "All her friends wish it and say they are capable of it, and having acted on Greek principles should have Greek exercises."

I might add that there is a firmly held, if factually unsubstantiated, belief in the Greek-American community today that the constitutional fathers actually debated making ancient Greek the language of the new republic.

Thus, my subject today is, broadly speaking, the Constitution of the United States. It is, I realize, a subject not unfamiliar to you, given that last year was the bicentennial of the Constitution. Of the two bicentennials we have marked in just over a decade, I regard the more recent as by far the more significant, and for this reason: although many countries have had revolutions and succeeded in establishing their independence, very few have been able to put into place—let alone sustain for two centuries—a constitution providing for free self-government and the rule of law.

Indeed, the hard-fought victory of the colonies over the British in the revolutionary war did not lead inevitably to the democratic nation whose freedoms and opportunities we are privileged, and I hope grateful, to enjoy today. On the contrary, the fruits of that victory could easily have been lost in the aftermath. It was in fact because of the sense that they were being lost that we had the Constitutional Convention of 1787. The outcome of that convention in Philadelphia over the summer of 1787 was anything but a foregone conclusion—either with respect to the terms of the proposed Constitution or with respect to the states' willingness to ratify it. Fortunately, the Constitution reflected the genius of the Founding Fathers—surely a most remarkable assemblage of men for any country at any time in history.

Over our evolution as a nation the Constitution has served as the glue that binds our country together. In most other countries the unity of the nation derives from a homogeneous population, or a common religion, or a shared cultural and social heritage extending back over the centuries. This is not true of the United States. When I was a boy my father, who came to this country as a young immigrant of fifteen, loved to tell me the story of Franklin Roosevelt's salutation to a delegation from the Daughters of the American Revolution—as they came in the door he greeted them: "Welcome, fellow immigrants." Our Constitution has made it possible to build a nation based on the principles of free self-government that includes people from every nation, of every culture, of every religious background, and of every race.

Despite the extraordinary wisdom and durability of our constitutional system, however, we saw it challenged even as the bicentennial was being celebrated. It is about that challenge that I would like now to speak for a few minutes. In the Iran/Contra affair, which I examined for most of last year as a member of the select committee, we have seen an effort by some to resolve the inherent tension over the respective roles of the Congress and the executive by circumventing established constitutional processes.

The Founding Fathers proceeded on a separation-of-powers principle, with its systems of checks and balances, both to create a deterrent to the abuse of power and to assure better policy through the interaction of executive and legislature. Actually what the Founding Fathers established was not so much a strict separation of powers as power-sharing by the separate branches.

As a result, policy must be made within the checks-and-balances guidelines set out in the Constitution. With respect to foreign policy, for example:

The president is commander-in-chief of the armed forces, but the Congress is charged with raising and supporting armies, providing and maintaining a navy, and declaring war.

The president has the authority to make treaties and appoint ambassadors, but that authority is qualified by the necessity for Senate advice and consent.

Congress has the power of the purse through the appropriations process. Should the president require financial resources to pursue a foreign policy initiative, he must come to Congress for the funding.

This last is not a theoretical proposition. The decision within the administration to seek support for the Contras outside the processes established by the Constitution, after the dispute between Congress and the president had been duly resolved against Contra funding in accordance with those processes, lies at the heart of the Iran/Contra affair. Persons in the executive branch circumvented the system of checks and balances. They dismissed the proposition that the system serves to deter abuse of power and to assure better policymaking.

What became apparent in that affair was a breakdown—or perhaps more accurately put, a deliberate breaking down—of the checks and balances at work between the Congress and the executive for two hundred years. What is more, a breakdown occurred even within the executive branch itself. A system was developed whereby decisions were made outside all established procedures. Elected officials, accountable to the citizenry, were excluded. Members of the cabinet, of the executive branch—confirmed by the Senate and accountable to Congress—were also excluded.

The testimony presented in the course of the Iran/Contra hearings revealed the establishment of a covert network to raise money for pursuing foreign policy objectives without the knowledge of Congress, ranking officials in the executive branch (notably the secretaries of state and defense), or the people, and often at odds with publicly declared policy objectives. A secret treasury was created by soliciting funds from foreign governments and private donors and by making profits on clandestine arms sales.

Underlying this extraordinary network were certain assumptions inimical to our constitutional system. They would, if unchecked, undermine the rights and freedoms our Constitution guarantees. Whereas our Constitution is premised on the proposition that all of us—without exception—live under law, the Iran/Contra network operated on the proposition that some people, if they hold certain views or feel strongly enough about them, are entitled to go above the law. In fact, in a moment of unusual frankness before the committee, one witness remarked: "Sometimes you have to go above the written law."

The argument was made that when convictions and beliefs are genuine, and when certain objectives are perceived as being in the nation's interest, then those objectives can be pursued regardless of contrary decisions made within the terms of the law and constitutional processes.

Yet that path leads to the subversion of democracy, not to its strengthening. Admiral Bobby Inman, the former head of the National Security Agency and deputy director of the CIA, gave a very different response when asked in a television interview about the matter. He said:

> My view is very direct. Once you have legislation that establishes a process, you have three alternatives: you get the law changed, if you think it's wrong; if you believe it's unconstitutional, you find a case and take it to the Supreme Court; or you comply with the law and work to make it work. I don't believe there's a legitimate option in a country of laws to simply go around it as the way you do business.

In a sense, Admiral Inman was merely restating what Socrates had to say in the Platonic dialogue, *The Crito*. There he imagines himself being cross-examined by the laws and constitution of Athens, and I quote:

> Look at it in this way. Suppose that while we were preparing to run away from here (or however one should describe it) the laws and constitution of Athens were to come and confront us and ask this question:
>
> "Now, Socrates, what are you proposing to do? Can you deny that by this act which you are contemplating you intend, so far as you have the power, to destroy us, the laws, and the whole state as well? Do you imagine that a city can continue to exist and not be turned upside down, if the legal judg-

ments which are pronounced in it have no force but are nullified and destroyed by private persons?"

I suggest that this one small dialogue from Plato should be made required reading for all who enter public service.

In his dissent in the *Olmstead* case Justice Brandeis recognized the danger that well-meaning people can pose to liberty. He warned that we should not focus on motives because "men born of freedom are naturally alert to repel invasion of their liberty by evil-minded rulers." We are alert to that. But then Justice Brandeis went on to say: "The greatest dangers to liberty lurk in insidious encroachment by men of zeal, well-meaning but without understanding."

That, I believe, is the central issue in the Iran/Contra affair. Zealots, convinced of the rightness of their cause, were prepared to go around, behind, over, and under established processes in order to achieve their objectives. But our constitution gives us a process for reaching decisions, for resolving differences among ourselves. It guarantees each of us the right to be heard, but it does not guarantee any one of us that our view will prevail. It guards for each of us the right to present our arguments while denying us the right to impose them on others. It proceeds on the premise that reasonable men and women may differ in good faith, and no one has a monopoly on truth.

It is worth remembering that while Thomas Jefferson and John Adams were often adversaries, they worked happily together on the Declaration of Independence, and collaborated in the great work of creating this nation.

Democracy is not a perpetual motion machine which, once having been set in motion, can be counted on to operate of its own accord. For democracy to work requires the active commitment of each succeeding generation. It presupposes a willingness on the part of the citizenry to get involved in the problems of their time, to participate rather than to criticize from the safe distance of the sidelines or to turn their backs.

The ancient Greeks looked very scornfully upon the man who was not deeply involved in his society. Our modern word *idiot* comes from the Greek word, *idiotes*, meaning a man who leads a completely private existence and contributes nothing to the common welfare. To them, such a person was neither useful nor truly happy, since happiness was regarded not as a passive sensation, but as satisfaction derived from public activity.

That is a truth we ignore at our peril. It is a truth the framers of the Constitution understood well. Perhaps you have heard the story of the last day of the Constitutional Convention, but it bears repeating. As the delegates were leaving Independence Hall after four months of deliberation, a woman in the crowd is said to have called out to Benjamin Franklin: "What is it to be, Dr. Franklin? A monarchy or a republic?"

And Benjamin Franklin replied: "A republic, madam, if you can keep it."

Franklin's charge uttered in the streets of Philadelphia two hundred years ago remains our challenge today. Stephen Brademas, deeply imbued with the values of his dual Greek and American heritage, understood this challenge and did all he could to meet it. It is on such contributions that the strength of American democracy rests.

The Art of Diplomacy
SIR PETER RAMSBOTHAM, G.C.M.C., G.C.V.O.

The Honorable Sir Peter Ramsbotham, former British ambassador to the United States, was educated at Eton and Magdalen College, Oxford. He served in World War II and on the Allied Control Commission in Berlin and Hamburg. In 1950, he joined the Foreign Office and saw service in London, New York, and Paris. After a sabbatical year at the Institute of Strategic Studies in London, he was appointed successively as British high commissioner in Nicosia, ambassador to Iran, ambassador to the United States, and governor of Bermuda.

Sir Peter is a director of Lloyds Bank and of the Commercial Union Assurance Company. He is also a trustee of the Leonard Cheshire Foundation and chairman of the Ryder-Cheshire Mission for the Relief of Suffering.

Sir Peter holds honorary degrees from Akron University, the College of William and Mary, the University of Maryland, and Yale University. He is a Knight of Saint John, as well as a Knight Grand Cross of the Order of Saint Michael and Saint George and Knight Grand Cross of the Royal Victorian Order.

SINCE MY SUBJECT IS a wide one, I must be selective. One could talk about the history of diplomacy, its origins and changes over the centuries—about the development of diplomatic theory, diplomatic language, and points of diplomatic procedure—all fascinating subjects, on which much has been written. Instead, I would like to say something about what we mean by the word *diplomacy*; to explain what are the qualifications required in a diplomat today—the qualities he is expected to display and the tasks he is called upon to perform. I shall illustrate my theme by drawing on my experience in dealing overseas with certain foreign governments and heads of state and noting the methods adopted in the conduct of their foreign policies. I shall be concentrating on the positive role of the diplomat in trying to promote international understanding; I believe that that aspect is too often ignored. I shall of course be giving a British view based on my experience in the British Foreign Service at home and abroad, though I have no doubt that most American diplomats will have had similar experiences.

There have been many definitions of diplomacy. It has been described as "a skill in the managing of international relations"; as "the art of negotiating agreements between sovereign states, with the purpose of creating international confidence"; as "the search for compromise through mutual concession in order to reconcile conflicting interests."

The word *diplomacy* is too often used loosely to mean a country's foreign policy, the strategy chosen by a government to promote and defend the country's interests and objectives abroad. A foreign policy is the business of a government, the province of statecraft, the product of a legislative and political process in a democracy. Diplomacy is subordinate to that. It is the execution of that policy, the means whereby the political strategy is achieved.

One of the reasons why there is this confusion between the formulation of a foreign policy and its execution is that the policy-makers often try to execute their own policies, instead of leaving that task to the professional diplomat, who is skilled in the art of negotiation and can also provide an element of continuity between changing governments and administrations. It is sometimes dangerous to let politicians take too personal a part in detailed negotiations: that can arouse public expectations and lead to misunderstandings. Moreover, the politician who can count on only a limited term of office can be tempted to seek short-term national advantages instead of negotiating for longer-term solutions. And most of the world's problems today don't offer quick solutions.

Of course, there are striking exceptions to this rule. Henry Kissinger, in my day, master-minded the making of U.S. foreign policies and also executed them, as in his Middle East shuttle diplomacy in the early 1970s. But then he was not a politician.

The work of the diplomat and the tools of his trade are difficult to define. In most of the disciplines you study at a university, there is usually a specific amount of knowledge, skill, or aptitude that you need to acquire in order to pursue a particular career or vocation—be it as a doctor, lawyer, engineer, scientist, or economist, or in one of the teaching professions. That statement is not true for those who seek to enter the administrative branch of the British Foreign Service. Certainly you need a good university degree, but it can be in any one of several disciplines. One of our more successful recent ambassadors took his degree in chemistry. Nor is the mastery of foreign languages a prerequisite for the Foreign Service. It is indeed useful, but, apart from a knowledge of French (still in many ways the diplomatic language), an aptitude to learn languages is all that is required; though, nowadays, after entry you are usually asked to undertake intensive training in some foreign language.

In other countries today—perhaps the majority of European countries—for entry into their foreign services, some legal training is usually required. This would seem to make sense, since the drafting of treaties and international agreements demands a trained legal mind. But in the British Foreign Service we have preferred to entrust this work to a team of legal advisers who specialize in international law. On the whole, I think our system is a good one. The legally trained mind can sometimes fail to see the forest for the trees. And nowadays, with the complexity and variety of international exchanges, it is, I think, best to seek the advice of experts. Indeed, many international negotiations today relate to financial, scientific, and technical subjects with which the professional diplomat cannot be familiar. He has then to be part of a negotiating team, but giving the overall direction. When I was a young diplomat we did not have to deal with so many of the kind of economic, technical, and scientific problems that the proliferation of international organizations, the astonishing increase in the number of independent nations since the war, and the extension of governmental interest and intervention have since brought about.

The modern diplomat has to be, if not a jack-of-all-trades, at least sufficiently flexible to deal sensibly with a broad range of activities and subjects. He is certainly not an amateur, in the rather pejorative sense that the word has acquired. He is more like a general practitioner in the medical profession, who spends his career accumulating experience and expertise and probably also establishing a reputation for knowledge of a particular subject or a particular part of the world.

Diplomacy is more a written than a verbal art. The diplomat must be able to grasp quickly arguments put forward by the specialist, to weigh conflicting views, and to bring them together with clear recommendations for a decision. He must learn to draft well, whether it be letters, dispatches, telegrams, or cabinet memoranda. He must be able to select and summarize, without losing clarity and balance. The pressure of work is fairly intensive, and there is little time for scholarly rumination. And he must write good sensible prose. Other people will then not only understand what he writes; they will also find it more acceptable for being expressed with some felicity in the choice of words.

And what are the *qualities* sought in a successful diplomat serving abroad? I cannot do better than quote from a recent article by a distinguished American ambassador—a friend of mine—describing the qualities necessary for successful diplomacy: "tolerance and integrity, the ability to inspire trust and confidence, experience and judgement in relating your country's interests to the nuances and realities of other cultures, and the ability to communicate effectively."[1]

And to these I would add: truthfulness, modesty, and patience (and nowadays, perhaps, courage, judging by the number of kidnappings and assassinations of diplomats). Truthfulness: there is always a temptation for an ambassador to report to his government what they would like to hear rather than what they ought to know. Modesty: the temptation here is for an ambassador to become too full of his own importance and thus an easy target for flattery. Above all, patience: he must resist the temptation of trying to secure a rapid diplomatic triumph before his mission comes to an end. Many of the most important international problems of the post-war era have taken several years to resolve.

Since the dictionary defines a diplomat as "an adroit negotiator," I ought to say something about the art of negotiation. But it is a skill that is acquired and practised in many other professions, especially in legal, financial, and business activities, and there are many books on the subject. It is not the speciality of a diplomat. Indeed, in one sense, we are all practical negotiators. When we differ, we use negotiation to reconcile our differences—whether between landlord and tenant over the rent or between husband and wife over the room temperature. We try to reach

---

[1] Carol Laise, "Diplomacy in a Changing Society," *Diplomacy for the Future* (Washington, D.C.: Georgetown University Press, 1987).

agreement when there are some interests that are shared and others that are opposed. It is the same for the diplomat, except that he is dealing exclusively in the public sector and with governments and their representatives.

The objective is simple and so are the guidelines. The purpose of diplomatic negotiation is not to win a victory; it is to try by mutual concession to reach some durable understanding. (I say durable, because to find permanent solutions to international problems is seldom possible.) The diplomatic negotiator has to find ways that will satisfy the legitimate needs of both sides. If the negotiation is to prove successful, both sides at the conclusion must feel they have gained. And in the vital field of defence negotiations (the SALT and INF Agreements, for example) each side must be assured of its own security at each step of a disarmament process. Neither side in a negotiation can expect to win all its objectives. Some compromise is necessary; otherwise it is not a negotiation. And the question always is at what point to accept a compromise. It has been well said that the art of diplomacy is to sense the time at which an idea that has proved to be non-negotiable can, because of changes in the many variables involved, be successfully "slipped into place." For example, with the recent rapprochement between Greece and Turkey the Cyprus problem may at last become negotiable.

But, whatever the forum or the protagonists, whether private individuals, business corporations, or sovereign governments, the ability to see the situation as the other side sees it is one of the most important skills a negotiator can possess. If you want to influence them, you must understand the power of their point of view.

I have spoken about the *qualifications* for, and the *qualities* sought in, the ideal diplomat. What of his *tasks*, the tasks of a diplomat today—say, an ambassador at his embassy abroad? In a conventional lecture on the subject one might list the tasks broadly as two-fold:

(a) explaining, promoting, and defending the interests of his country and exercising powers of persuasion in negotiation for particular objectives, and
(b) analysing events, identifying trends, forecasting developments, and reporting his conclusions to his government, with recommendations, where appropriate, for policy decisions.

But I would like to add a third requirement and perhaps today the most important, namely

(c) trying to understand and explain to his own government the attitudes, impulses, and idiosyncracies of the country where he is posted, so as to ensure that his government does not make a move that will prove to be "counterproductive."

In short, he has a contribution to make toward better international understanding.

Since the idea that international understanding needs expert care and attention is perhaps not readily accepted, it is important to define the positive role of the diplomat in trying to achieve it.

"International understanding" has a wide connotation, extending beyond the immediate world of diplomacy to something broader and less definable. It has to do with the perception that the people of two countries have of each other. It is, if you like, though on a much larger scale, comparable to the understanding or lack of understanding that in our societies and communities we have of each other.

If I say "the Chinese" or "the South Africans" or "the Italians" or "the Jamaicans," one has at once a certain image or some association of thoughts and judgments about the peoples and the governments of those countries, derived partly from personal experience—where one has travelled, whom one has met—and partly from what one has read in the press or seen on the television. We do our best with, inevitably, a pretty sketchy knowledge of what it really means to be Chinese, South African, Italian, or Jamaican. We have to form our judgments about foreign countries and their peoples from a fragmentary collection of bits of history remembered from school, the odd acquaintance with this or that foreign national, or perhaps a visit abroad, although we may not speak their language or read their newspapers. Much of our judgments of other countries and their peoples is given to us ready-made by the newspapers, television, and their foreign correspondents. It is often their judgments that make up what is known as "public opinion" in respect of what is happening overseas.

The fact is, of course, that it is only comparatively recently that our "public" has had any "opinion" at all about overseas events. Before the Great War of 1914, "the public" was largely uninterested in the principles of foreign policy or in the methods by which that policy was executed. International affairs were regarded as a specialist study, best left to the government and its experts. Even in an island kingdom like Britain, which depended upon world trade for her prosperity, knowledge of what was really going on abroad was confined to a few. For instance, it has been said that in 1890 the British foreign secretary, Lord Salisbury, in a deal with Bismarck, exchanged Heligoland for Zanzibar without properly informing the British cabinet.

In our own lifetimes, at least up to the last war, a few great powers dominated world affairs. The League of Nations, the precursor of the United Nations, comprised then no more than a handful of countries—mostly European; and international affairs were the province of a small class of professionals.

But three phenomena have changed all this: the advent of the atom bomb, the expansion of the U.N. and the third world, and the increasing role and influence of the media, combined with the speed of international communications.

Not so long ago there was still a direct relationship between power and influence in international affairs. A

British government in the late nineteenth century could send a gunboat off the coast of an antagonistic country and its government would change its policies. Today, things are different. The possibility of escalating a small clash of conventional arms into a global nuclear war has brought new and powerful restraints. The United States, possessing the most powerful armory the world has ever seen, had the greatest difficulty during the Cuban crisis of 1962, in preventing a distant power—Russia—from planting missiles on its very doorstep. That would have been inconceivable fifty years ago.

The astonishing expansion of the U.N. has reinforced this divorce between power and influence. Today the U.N. comprises more than 150 different countries, the majority having only recently acquired independence, with the breakup of the great colonial empires. Their votes bear no relation to the amount of power that can be exercised or the degree of responsibility that can be assumed.

All nations, weak and strong, have been affected by this phenomenon. Britain and France experienced it at Suez, and even the two superpowers have to pay attention to it. But peace cannot simply be preserved by voting in the U.N. Until such time as there is a world federal union or a universally accepted rule of law, those nations that possess effective power must retain the primary responsibility for preserving world peace—exercising that responsibility, one would hope, under the restraints imposed by the nuclear deterrent and by the U.N., however imperfect it may be.

There has been another development to add to the difficulties with which the modern diplomat has to contend. Whereas previously, international relations were largely governed by the interplay of purely national interests, pursued in terms of a balance of power—mostly the shifting alliances between the European nations—and through bilateral forms of diplomacy, today, ideological, moral, and emotional factors have come to influence foreign relations; and they find a sounding box in the forum of the U.N. and other bodies where multilateral diplomacy has replaced the traditional bilateral mode of diplomacy.

The clash between the communist ideology and the desire of Western democracies to defend individual liberties has dominated the post-war scene; but no less important have been the emotional forces behind the urge of third world countries—the underdeveloped, the non-aligned—to overcome their traditional handicaps and to find ways and means of exercising their own influence in the world. The latest of such forces to appear is the emotional thrust of Islam.

The third phenomenon that has complicated the task of the diplomat is the increasing role and influence of the media. Today it is all-pervading—especially the TV coverage and reporting of international events. In open societies, like the United States and Europe, the making of foreign policy, and its execution—the diplomatic arm—have come increasingly under the pressure of public opinion and hence the media. Moreover, with the growing interdependence among the nations of what we call the Western world—financial, monetary, scientific interdependence—the distinction between predominantly domestic and predominantly foreign matters has become less sharp. And this tendency has led to a blurring of the lines between internal and external issues—again enhancing the influence of the media on foreign affairs.

There are, of course, dangers here. Although the elaboration of a nation's foreign policy should, as we have seen, be to a large extent a public process, subject to all the democratic procedures of an open society, the conduct of that foreign policy should not be regarded as a legitimate field for public scrutiny. And unless some degree of confidentiality is preserved in diplomatic exchanges, we in the West will be at a disadvantage in negotiating with the closed societies of the Eastern block or the more authoritarian regimes in the third world.

Because of these post-war phenomena, the diplomat today is called upon to assess, understand, and form judgments on far more complex matters than his more traditional predecessor. How is he to advise his government on the policies or attitudes that should be adopted? Let me give you two comparatively recent examples of such difficult judgments.

Why did the Russians invade Afghanistan in 1979? Was it part of a movement of expansion intended to reach eventually to the warm waters of the Gulf and the Indian Ocean and so control the oil resources of the Middle East? Or was it the outcome of a secret power struggle in the Kremlin—the manifestation of the military gaining power over the politiburo? Or did the Soviet rulers think they could exploit the West's weaknesses and the turmoil in Southwest Asia at that time, and turn it to their own advantage? Or was it—as I thought at the time—because they had little alternative, believing that the upsurge of Islam and the imminent overthrow of a puppet regime in Afghanistan could dangerously infect the millions of Muslim people within the Soviet Union's own borders? Which was the right interpretation? Or was it a mixture of several reasons? At the time there were champions of each of these interpretations among the foreign correspondents of the Western media.

My second example is taken from the same part of the world and the same year. Why was the shah of Iran overthrown in 1979, taking by surprise the Western governments that had been giving him so much support and, for a quarter of a century, praising his achievements for his country and his defence of Western interests? Were we fooled by the shah during those years? Was he really the arch villain, a cruel dictator, as he has since been portrayed? Or were the forces of Islam, dormant for centuries, suddenly reanimated beyond control? Or did the shah become too arrogant, believing he could do no wrong and deceiving himself that his people really appreciated his reforms? Or had he lost control over the divisive social effects of a steadily rising inflation, brought about by the sudden influx of wealth from the quadrupling of the price of oil, which he himself had been the first to champion in 1973–74?

It is never easy at the time to find the correct answers to such questions. But it is the ambassador's job to draw together all the threads and search for the right understanding of such events, so that his government can formulate the best response. I know only too well how difficult it is fully to understand what is really going on in a foreign country even though, as ambassador, one may be living and travelling in that country, meeting a wide range of people, and served by a diplomatic staff who speak the language and know the people.

A knowledge of the history of other countries is a great help toward a better understanding of what is happening, what is likely to happen, and what are the significant influences. Many international incidents, indeed wars, have been caused by the failure of the government of one country to understand the significant influences behind the foreign policy decisions of another country; or a government's reacting, through fear, to what was wrongly perceived to be an aggressive move or, on the other hand, failing to perceive an aggressive move until it was too late (e.g., Hitler's invasion of the Rhineland).

The Western attitude toward the Soviet Union has been ambivalent. Sometimes "we have seemed to believe that Soviet hostility is endemic, the emotional product of Russian antagonism—and to be dealt with only by forceful confrontation. At other times, we seem to regard the Soviet Union as a mirror image of the West, and to believe that their latent liberal tendencies can be encouraged and released by the West's more accommodating attitudes."[2] We should pay heed to what Gorbachev said last December in his interview with Tom Brokaw of NBC: "The U.S.A. should learn a little about Russia before passing judgments on this country—you cannot understand our actions if you don't know our history."

Oliver Cromwell, when arranging for the education of his son, Richard, said to the schoolmaster, "I would have him learn a little history." Your great historian, Professor Dumas Malone, writing of Thomas Jefferson and his contemporaries and comparing them with modern statesmen, said, "They thought more about the future and they knew more about the past."

If we are to understand other nations, other peoples, we must learn what their history has been, what are the physical constraints and stimulants of their environment, how long they have enjoyed what we call the advantages of a civilized society, what the religious influences may be, and the ideals and objectives they hold dear, which may well not be the same as our own. We must be willing to listen to and respect the views and interests of other nations.

A historical perspective will help one to understand that nations can be divided one from another not only by space, but also by time. It is not rewarding to expect the many new nations in Africa and Asia to pay the same regard to what we call democratic principles of government, when it has taken us seven hundred years to evolve our own democratic institutions out of the first parliamentary assemblies in England in the thirteenth century. The historians of the future may, indeed, find reason to question some of the standards and practices that we in our modern society regard as decent and progressive; as we too may find it difficult to understand how liberal and imagi-

---

[2]James Billington, "Diplomacy in the Soviet Union," *Diplomacy for the Future* (Washington, D.C.: Gerogetown University Press, 1987).

native men in the early nineteenth century saw nothing wrong in keeping slaves.

Or—a more modern example of mutual misunderstanding—think how difficult it must be for young Israelis today, with decades of persecution and violence behind them, to understand that a Palestinian youth may see membership in the P.L.O. as a patriotic duty no less honorable for him than membership in the Israeli Army for an Israeli youth. The same distorted vision lies behind the relationship between Turkish Cypriots and the Greek Cypriots; and certainly the same is true in Northern Ireland.

To try to understand other peoples and the motives of foreign governments does not mean that we also have to approve or excuse whatever they do. *Tout comprendre* is not *tout pardonner*. Dishonesty, selfishness, greed, and aggression are no less reprehensible among the rulers of nations than they are among individuals (Khomeini and Ghadafi). But if we wish to further the cause of peace in the world, we must first try to understand why other peoples and their governments behave as they do.

I have to acknowledge that the skills of the diplomat count for less today in our open societies in the West—especially in Europe, where interdependence and international co-operation have been increasing with the evolution of the European Economic Community (EEC). National barriers are being removed, and new forms of multilateral diplomacy are being devised to handle the mutual affairs of the twelve European member states. The old national antagonisms, which led to wars between them, are no longer thinkable.

But, just as nationalism is retreating in Europe, it seems to be increasing in parts of what we call the third world—and even inside the Soviet Union's vast empire of Asian peoples with their differing historical and religious backgrounds. The European colonial systems in the Middle East, Africa, and Asia, whatever their failings, at least provided an element of international stability in the world. Today there is an unstable vacuum of power where regional and national rivalries can threaten to draw the bigger powers into local wars. I would argue that our professional diplomat today has most to offer in dealing with authoritarian or nationalistic regimes—the closed societies of the communist-controlled countries, or the autocratic governments in the third world, which are dominated by all-powerful heads of state, dominant figures in the history of their countries, who can in their lifetime change the pattern of international relations. It is important to understand the forces that motivate such men and try to anticipate their objectives and their next moves.

By way of illustration, I have chosen three enlightened autocrats—General de Gaulle in France, Archbishop Makarios in Cyprus, and the shah of Iran—with all of whom I had professional dealings—and to examine their chosen methods for promoting the interests of their countries. For in each we have a head of state who was powerful enough to devise and execute his own foreign policy.

In 1962, the British Foreign Office sent me to Paris as the senior political councellor at our embassy, at the time of the rise to power of a spectacular enlightened autocrat, de Gaulle. He restored to France her self-confidence, after years of humiliation and self-doubt under the Fourth Republic. At the time many of us were baffled by his seemingly strange and arbitrary actions. We should not have been. For many years he had been publicly revealing his political philosophy and strategy in a series of remarkable books which few foreigners bothered to read. Like Machiavelli's prince, de Gaulle described the attributes of the leader. The prescription was mystery, surprise, pride, and ruthlessness. The harsh and the brutal combined with charm, elegance, and wit—a deliberately contrived mixture. He was incapable of compromise in pursuit of French interests. His guiding passion was to extol and extend

France's position in the world. There was for de Gaulle no morality, no sentiment in international relations. Nationalism, he thought, was the most enduring political force, and interdependence was a deception. Although he paid lip service to the concept of the European Economic Community twenty-five years ago, he would surely have resisted the breakdown of national barriers in Europe that we are witnessing today. As a medium power which had suffered a decline, France needed an active diplomacy to compensate for what previously she had achieved by weight of resources. De Gaulle saw the actors on the world stage as the nations, constantly in movement; and it was in knowing how to exploit these movements that France's opportunities were conceived to lie. France, he believed, could only hope to assert her maximum influence by being free to maneuver between the great powers and their respective clients, sometimes as ally, sometimes as adversary. His was a version of the classical idea of the balance of power. In the nineteenth century Britain was a master at this game, the object being so to shift one's weight in a network of changing alliances as to ensure that no other power gained domination in Europe—a form of international judo if you like. De Gaulle was the twentieth-century champion of that game, and no one has played it so well since. It required finesse, nerve, and quickness of anticipation. France could, he believed, only achieve her ambitions in situations of international flux. It was no coincidence that de Gaulle began asserting himself only in 1962. Before then he was stuck with the Algerian problem, and the great powers were frozen in static confrontation by the Berlin crisis. But with the advent of the Vietnam War and the Sino-Soviet split, France acquired a new liberty of action.

It was just bad luck that Britain had made her first bid to enter the European Economic Community when de Gaulle, for the first time, had his hands free to stop us. It was an exciting time then, I remember, negotiating for our entry into Europe. The French strove hard to make the terms of entry incompatible with Britain's interests—the British Commonwealth ties or sterling as an international currency. And each time we found a way round in the negotiations, until, at length, de Gaulle was obliged to exercise a flat political veto to keep us out. Eleven years had to pass before we could join Europe.

How different would have been Britain's and Europe's history over the past twenty-five years if we had been able to avoid that veto in 1962. I think now, in retrospect, that we might have done so had we fully understood at the time de Gaulle's deep-seated fears and aspirations. But we would have had to convince him that, in certain circumstances, we would be prepared to support an essentially European point of view, even in the face of American disapproval.

So much for the greatest of the modern enlightened autocrats. Then in 1969 the Foreign Office sent me to Cyprus as British high commissioner to try to work toward a settlement of the dispute between the Greek and Turkish Cypriots—that is to say of "the Cyprus problem," dominated for so long by the figure of Archbishop Makarios.

Archbishop Makarios—"His Beatitude," as he was called—was an engaging personality. He was a truly Byzantine character, both devious and profound and with a splendid sense of humor that served him well when things got rough. He was elected archbishop at the early age of thirty-seven and dominated the scene for twenty-five years. No other political leader emerged to challenge his ascendancy. Half dedicated priest, half wily politician, he kept Cyprus in a perpetually uneasy balance between Greece and Turkey, whose rivalry in the Eastern Mediterranean perpetuated the sad division of Greek and Turkish Cyprus. Centuries of experience under foreign occupation had taught the Greek Cypriots how to profit from their own weaknesses. Like de Gaulle, Makarios perfected the art of international

The Art of Diplomacy 143

judo, playing one interest off against another, never allowing himself to become beholden to a stronger power, not even to the U.N., but ever ready to enhance his own importance by making a nuisance of himself while taking care not to provoke too hostile a reaction.

The extent of his implication with the EOKA movement in the 1950s has never been proven, but there is good evidence that he gave his approval to the murderous tactics against the British forces in Cyprus in 1955, and later in 1963, against the Turkish Cypriots.

It was hard for the British to forget that. And yet, in dealing with Makarios, one had to understand that he was not only the archbishop of Cyprus—and in fact he devoted a surprisingly large amount of his time to the church—but also the ethnarch of Cyprus. Every archbishop in Cyprus for two hundred years had also been a political leader by virtue of his office and, as such, Makarios regarded it as his traditional role to lead his people in resistance to the "occupying foreign power."

He also became the elected president of Cyprus—an independent republic created almost overnight in 1960. I think he genuinely felt himself to be above party—to be the national, as well as the spiritual, leader of his people. But he had little conception of the political role of a president as distinct from ethnarch.

During my time in Cyprus the sensibilities of the Turkish Cypriots were constantly being offended by his government, to a degree that indicated either deliberate provocation or poor judgment of the Turkish character. Makarios and his cabinet of Greek Cypriots made things harder for the Turkish Cypriot community to co-operate as the junior partner in the economic and administrative life of the country. And for their part, the Turkish Cypriots did little to lessen the fears of their Greek compatriots that they were secretly working for partition and the creation of a Turkish state within Cyprus. It was these inherent attitudes that made the prospects of an intercommunal settlement so remote.

If Makarios had handled the Turkish Cypriots with as much shrewdness and statesmanship as he displayed in arguing his case at the U.N. or in preserving Cyprus from the pressures of the Greek junta in Athens, things might have been very different. He was, I believe, a genuine Cypriot patriot, as patriotism is understood in Cyprus. And he was determined, despite many calculated hints to the contrary, never to allow an effective union (enosis) of Cyprus with Greece.

Had we—the British and Americans—understood better his impulses and motives regarding enosis, we might have found some form of *modus vivendi*—perhaps a loose confederation; indeed at one time I thought I had found the right formula. But the time was not then ripe for any solution.

Whatever criticisms can be levelled against Makarios, his commanding presence and his genius for political and physical survival helped to preserve an uneasy peace in the Eastern Mediterranean for a long span of years.

I did my best to understand his complex character. Like most people, he was a mixture of strengths and weaknesses. I found him a fascinating person and enjoyed my dealings with him. It will be many years before Cyprus will again find a leader of his stature.

Well, after Cyprus, I thought I had had enough of enlightened autocrats. But the Foreign Office, in its wisdom, decided in 1971 to send me as British ambassador to Iran, to the court of the shah of Persia, the greatest of all modern autocrats. I got to know him quite well. His later fate was a tragedy. It need not have happened, if he had not tried to bring Iran into the twentieth century within his own lifetime—and if we, in the West, had not uncritically abetted him in his ambitions.

The Art of Diplomacy

When I arrived in Iran, the shah was at the height of his power. He had broken the might of the feudal landlords and given land to the peasants by setting up rural cooperatives. He had emancipated the women—an advance now sadly reversed by Khomeini—introduced the first social services, reduced the rate of illiteracy, and transformed Iran into a semi-industrial state, all within fifteen years.

But he was too proud, too ambitious, and in too much of a hurry. His image was all-pervading. Every achievement was attributed personally to the shah's wisdom or to the shah's intervention. A new water supply to a remote mountain village was seldom ascribed to the efforts of the provincial governor, but to the shah personally.

I remember once during a lengthy conversation—he used I think to enjoy summoning me at inconvenient hours to one of his several palaces—when he was complaining of the ingratitude of his people, pointing out, as tactfully as I could, that the day might come when, instead of being lauded by his people for benefits he had not personally conferred, he would be criticized for failures he had equally not merited.

The Persians are a most attractive people, proud of a culture and civilization much older than our own. They are a nation of poets, but their lively imaginations quickly breed suspicion where there is no cause. Indeed, there are moderate and intelligent Persians today who have brought themselves to believe that, for some complicated reason, the British and U.S. governments conspired to bring Khomeini to power in Iran. In all this the shah was typical. Many were the occasions when I would have to listen to a tirade against some program on the BBC mildly critical of Iran or to his suspicious interpretation of some perfectly innocent event. He was a lonely man and trusted no one. He felt a need to assert his power by ruthless decisions. Every six years or so, he would sack his top admirals to ensure that there would be no potential usurpers in the armed forces. But such demonstrations of supreme power, with no sympathetic political or social support behind it, depended on the shah's retaining a strong will to make swift decisions. And already, in 1974, I believe, he had contracted cancer, and this gradually sapped his energy and his will.

Like de Gaulle and Makarios before him, the shah both invented and conducted his own foreign policy. His ambassadors were little more than messenger boys. He had visions of making Iran a highly industrialized country, financed by its increasing oil revenues and even attaining the position of a middle-ranking power, holding the balance between the Mediterranean and the Indian Ocean. It was a chimaera, but we in the West failed to discourage him in his lofty visions, so important to us was his strong commitment to the Western defence alliance, seeing Iran as a bastion against any Soviet advances.

Here we have the supreme autocrat, who had by his own efforts, for better or worse, changed the destiny of his country. Could his ultimate fate have been avoided if we had understood better his character, his ambition, and his preoccupations? Could we have anticipated the relatively sudden surge of apparently popular feeling, which swept Iran and brought Khomeini to power? I have posed some of these questions earlier in this talk. In my last dispatch from Tehran I did warn that the mullahs were beginning to feel disaffected by the rapid Westernization of the country.

For the shah, I think there was a time—probably about 1976—when the Americans and British might have been able—if we had exerted sufficient pressure—to persuade him to go further than he thought safe in introducing more realistic forms of constitutional and democratic government. But he was a very touchy and proud man and quickly resented any interference in Iran's domestic affairs. Certainly we failed to appreciate in time the degree of disappointment and disaffection among certain sections of the population and the extraordinary latent powers of some of the mullahs to exploit this.

Well, there you have a small portrait gallery of twentieth-century autocrats, each different in his own way, but each a catalyst of change in his country's history. There is no special link or logical connection between them. I have presented them to you because they became for me, each in his turn, central and significant points of reference at different periods of my diplomatic career, and also because each was larger than life, with a style of autocracy peculiar to himself.

I hope they have served to illustrate my themes—the significance of remarkable personalities, who emerge from time to time to dominate events and alter the course of history; the importance of studying and analysing the motives and methods of foreign governments; the influential role of the professional diplomat today, particularly in dealing with authoritarian and nationalistic regimes; and the need to recognize historical differences, so that we can more effectively promote international understanding.

The Continuity of Greek Culture

BERNARD M. W. KNOX

Bernard M. W. Knox, professor emeritus of classics at Harvard University, was born in Bradford, England, and educated at St. John's College, Cambridge, and Yale University. He served in World War II and received the Bronze Star and the Croix de Guerre. In 1947, he became a member of the Yale faculty and served for fourteen years before assuming the directorship of the Center for Hellenic Studies in Washington, D.C. He has also held appointments as visiting lecturer at the University of California at Berkeley and at Oxford University.

Professor Knox has been awarded a number of honors. He has been the recipient of a Guggenheim Fellowship, an award for literature from the National Institute for Arts and Letters, and the George Jean Nathan Award for Dramatic Criticism. He is the distinguished author of the well-known *Oedipus at Thebes, The Heroic Temper,* an acting version of *Oedipus the King,* and a number of articles.

M Y TITLE IS obviously over-ambitious. The continuity of Greek culture is a vast and complex field of study, demanding of its practitioners expertise in ancient, Byzantine, and modern Greek language, literature, and history, in Slavic and Turkish language and history, in the ritual and theology of the Orthodox Church, and a score of related disciplines, more in fact than one scholar can master in a lifetime. It is also an area of continuing interest and controversy. As recently as 1981, for example, the Hellenic Cultural Centre in London organized a panel discussion on the theme "3000 Years of Greek Identity." The three panels, chaired by the Byzantine scholar Robert Browning, were addressed by three Greeks brought up outside Greece, three Greeks raised in Greece, and three English scholars: one of the talks by Costa Carras, "3000 Years of Greek Identity—Myth or Reality?" was published in London in 1983. And it is a field in which fresh data are constantly supplied to feed fresh discussion.

Even in one narrow field, the continuity of the language, Professor Shipp, an Australian scholar who is a noted authority on the language of Homer, published a book entitled *Modern Greek Evidence for the Ancient Greek Vocabulary;* and in 1974 Nikolaus Andriotis, working in the opposite direction, published in Vienna his *Lexicon der Archaismen in neugriechischen Dialekten.* Here indeed are to be found three thousand years, or more, of Greek identity. The language inscribed on the fire-baked clay tablets found at Pylos on the mainland and at Knossos on Crete, dating from about 1600 B.C., is recognizably a primitive form of the language in which the newspapers of Athens are written today. Of course, in this immense stretch of time, the language has undergone many changes, but no other European language even comes close to claiming such a longevity; the only real parallel, in fact, is Chinese.

The profusion of studies published on this and all the other aspects of the long Greek tradition is such that any deluded speaker who thinks he can build a bridge between ancient and modern Greece in a forty-five-minute lecture will end up constructing a shaky structure at best and may find himself lamenting, like bridge builders in the famous medieval Greek ballad:

ἀλίμονο στους κόπους μας, κρῖμα στη δούλεψή μας
ὁλομερὶς να χτίζουμε, τὸ βράδυ να γκρεμειέται

Alas for our trouble, alas for our work,
To build it all day long, and have it collapse at night.

I shall aim lower. What I would like to do is to speak about my own encounter with modern Greece, its language and culture, the encounter of a classical literary scholar, brought up in Homer and Sophocles, with the Greece of Karamanlis and Papandreou (the elder Papandreou I may add—I first went to Greece in 1958). I should begin by explaining that I grew up in England, where I learned ancient Greek at school in London and then went on to St. John's College in Cambridge to read classics in the early thirties of this century.

The training I received was rigidly linguistic in emphasis (and in that was quite typical). The method seemed to have been designed with an eye to producing scholars who could write near-perfect Platonic prose and correct (but dull) Sophoclean iambic verse. I went through three years of Cambridge with the general impression that all the Greek worth reading came to a full stop with Theocritus (though there was of course the New Testament, but *that* was something for people studying Divinity) and furthermore that Greek history came to a stop with the death of Alexander the Great in 323 B.C. (after that it was Hellenistic history). Toward the end of my career at Cambridge I discovered that a friend of mine, who had chosen archaeology as his special field and was on his way to the British School in Athens, was studying, from a German handbook (there wasn't one in English), modern Greek. After talking to him and looking at the book I asked my tutor whether perhaps an acquaintance with modern Greek might be useful. "Not only will it not be useful," he said, "—the only people who use it are archaeologists who have to go there—not only will it not be useful, it will corrupt your prose style, and you will end up writing Greek that sounds like Polybius."

This Olympian disdain for people who actually went to modern Greece and who didn't *have* to go there was no new thing: in the spring of 1877 Oscar Wilde, then an undergraduate reading "Greats" at Magdalen College Oxford, went on a trip to Greece with Professor Mahaffy of his former college, Trinity College Dublin; they saw the excavations at Olympia, the temple at Bassae, Argos, Aegina, and Athens. Unfortunately for Wilde, he got back to Oxford three weeks late for the beginning of term (there were no jets in those days). "Voyages to Greece," says his biographer Richard Ellman, "were not common in the seventies of the last century. That they were necessary to a classical course in Oxford was more than Magdalen was ready to concede." Wilde was temporarily suspended for the rest of the academic year and deprived of his scholarship money. "I was sent down from Oxford," he said later, "for being the first undergraduate to visit Olympia."

This attitude, however, was not confined to the English classical establishment. Some time in the early *sixties* of this century I asked a French archaeologist who had spent most of his life in Greece at the Ecole Française whether he read the modern Greek poets. (I had just discovered, with immense excitement, the poetry of Kavafis and Seferis). "No," he said, "I have to know enough modern Greek to talk to the workmen on the dig, but I try to keep my acquaintance with it to a minimum—it might spoil my appreciation of the subtleties of Plato's style."

And I am sorry to say that this attitude toward modern Greek and modern Greece, typical of so many scholars, especially those concerned with literature, was just as prevalent in the United States when I first began to do graduate work and then to teach at Yale after the second World War. My colleagues spent their summers and their sabbatical years in London, Paris, Vienna, Rome—cities where there were manuscripts of ancient Greek authors to collate, where the great libraries offered immense bibliographical resources, the great cities their comforts and cultural amenities, and the universities their classical scholars for consultation and discussion. I, too, when my first fellowship allowed me to travel, in 1953, went to Rome and Florence, partly because, as a result of military service in Italy in the second World War, I spoke Italian, but also because in Florence the Biblioteca Laurenziana held the great manuscript of Sophocles, on whom I was working at the time. Greece was a place to visit, perhaps, but not to stay in (like New York); those scholars who did go contented themselves with a visit to the most important classical sites. They returned to their universities not so much disillusioned (for they had expected very little) as confirmed in their conviction that between the Greece of Pericles and Sophocles on the one hand and that of Venizelos and Seferis on the other (not that they knew very much about either of these two) there was a gap so wide that little or nothing of value to the classicist was to be learned from a closer knowledge of the life, literature, and language of modern Greece.

To the Greeks themselves, whose early training and later study reinforced their consciousness of the continuity of the Greek tradition, such an attitude must appear bizarre, just as it would appear strange to Englishmen if a foreign scholar of Chaucer or Shakespeare found nothing useful for his studies in the language and customs of modern England. But this attitude exists and persists, and since I too shared it to some extent before I had the good fortune to spend a whole year in Greece I would like to describe it and try to explain it. I have long since been free of it, but the converted heretic is perhaps the most competent authority on the beliefs he has rejected.

To begin with, there is the look of the place. No one can fail to be overwhelmed by the beauty and mystery of the Altis at Olympia by moonlight, or of Delphi at any hour (any hour that is when there are not ten thousand tourists taking pictures), and no one can fail to be impressed by the huge yet delicate beauty of the theater at Epidaurus, the long gallery in the fortress at Tiryns, the splendid yet somehow haunted site of Agamemnon's palace at Mycenae, and the tomb of the Athenian and Plataean dead on the plain where "Marathon looks on the sea." But these are secluded ancient sites, where the scholar can easily imagine himself in the Greece of classical or archaic times. The rest of Greece, however, is another kettle of fish. The scholar of Greek literature who manages to find his way behind the Larisa Station to what was Kolonos Hippios, with the marvelous lines of Sophocles ringing in his ears,

> εὐίππου ξένε, τᾶσδε χώρας
> ἵκου τὰ κράτιστα γᾶς ἔπαυλα,
> τὸν ἀργῆτα Κολωνόν, ἔνθ'
> ἁ λίγεια μινύρεται
> . . . ἀηδών . . .
>
> *(Oedipus at Colonus*, ll. 668 ff.)

> "Stranger, you have come to the land of fine horses, to earth's fairest home, white Colonus, where the nightingale, a permanent guest, trills her clear notes in green glades, amid the wine-dark ivy in the gods' sacred wood, heavy with fruit and berries, shaded from the sun, shielded from wind and weather."

is in for a terrible shock; what he will find at the end of the bus ride has little to do with horses and still less to do with nightingales. And suppose he tries to follow Socrates and Phaedrus out to the shady spot where they talked by the river Ilissos.

> This plane tree is spreading and tall [says Plato's Socrates] and there is a lovely shade from the high branches of the agnus; now that it is in full flower, it will make the place fragrant. And what a lovely

stream under the plane tree! and how cool to the feet . . . and the freshness of the air and the shrill summery music of the cicadas. And as a crowning delight this grass, thick on the gentle slope, just right to rest your head on it most comfortably.

Our scholar will be a very clever man if he can find the Ilissos at all and a very disappointed one if he does. Reluctantly, dodging traffic at every intersection, he makes his way back to the Acropolis, where, even though it is scarred and broken, there is enough left of the Parthenon and the Propylaea to remind him of the glories of Periclean Athens.

Outside Athens things are not much better. Our scholar's first view of Salamis and the straits in which the Greek fleet, watched by Xerxes from his throne, routed and sank the Persian galleys, will probably include the rusting hulks lying at anchor off Skaramangas; and all the way to the site of the Eleusinian Mysteries at Eleusis he will have to look at the plume of white smoke from the huge Herakles cement factory. Where are the pine trees on the Theban mountains, the haunts of Dionysos and his maenads, of nymphs and satyrs? Where is the narrow pass that Leonidas and his three-hundred Spartans held against the Persian hordes? (It would take an army corps to hold it now.) Where are the bees of Hymettos? The birds of Aristophanes? The seven gates of Thebes? Only in the books the scholar knows so well and to which he returns with relief. The first impressions of modern Greece, and particularly Athens, are enough to convince most scholars that they will understand the culture and literature of the fifth century B.C. much better working in a study in Oxford or New Haven than they ever will sitting in a *kafeneion* near Plateia tis Omonoias or riding the bus to Levadia.

Then there are the people, the Greeks themselves. To the visiting scholar they are the kindest and most solicitous of hosts (particularly in the country, where their hospitality can be overwhelming), hard-working, honest and admirable people; but, thinks the scholar, they don't *look* like the ancient Greeks. He has come to Greece for the first time with the idealized faces of the young men on the Parthenon frieze stamped on his memory, his mind full of Homeric tags like *xanthos Menelaos*, a phrase which, particularly if he is of Anglo-Saxon or Germanic stock, he has been taught to translate "blond Menelaos." In Athens he finds himself in a world of men and women who seem to be a startling contrast to the ideal faces that have haunted the imagination since he first saw them in the British Museum—of people who bear no resemblance to the gods and goddesses whose exquisitely proportioned features, set in the eternity of marble gilded by time, first drew him to his lifelong study of Greek.

And finally there is the language. He knows that it has changed somewhat in 2,500 years but still feels a certain confidence. After all, he has often successfully plowed his way through scholarly articles in modern Greek and occasionally read with some understanding a Greek newspaper bought in New York or London. Armed with his many years of study of ancient Greek and perhaps a few days on the boat devoted to a modern Greek phrase book, he expects to be able to manage fairly well when he gets there; after all, he has been studying Greek all his life. But the first contact with spoken Greek, especially if the speaker is a Piraeus taxi driver, can be a shattering experience. The visiting professor is reduced, like all his ignorant fellow passengers, to conducting his negotiations for a ride to Athens in what passes among Piraeus taxi drivers for English. Later, after buying a grammar and making a serious stab at the language, he begins to make some progress, but he realizes with growing despair that the reason he could read the scholarly articles and newspapers is that they are written in a Greek that tries to preserve as much of the ancient language as possible, whereas the waiters and bus drivers and policemen with whom he has to deal on his travels seem to be talking a different language. Modern Greek seems to have so little connection with the language of Demosthenes (Good Lord, it hasn't even got an *infinitive*) that he sees no point in trying to learn it.

On my first visit to Greece, once comfortably ensconced in a hotel in Iannina (we had arrived on a ferry from Brindisi to Igoumenitza) I displayed my knowledge of Greek by translating the headlines of the newspaper to my wife. But the balloon was soon punctured when she said: "Since you seem to know the language so well, why don't you call up and get us two more pillows and one more towel?" The language of Sophocles and Aristophanes was no help: my best effort—*pherete mou ena linon kai duo proskephalaia*—was answered by a series of excited questions that, unfortunately, I could not understand, and I was reduced to the expedient of going down to the desk and using sign language.

These first impressions are of course my own; but I am sure, from comparing notes with colleagues, that they are fairly representative. Unfortunately not many scholars of ancient Greek literature have the opportunity that was offered to me—to stay on for a whole year and find that these first impressions, like most first impressions, were unreliable.

First, the land itself. It is true that the country has changed enormously since the fifth century, but we forget that many of the things we complain of were already a cause for concern in ancient times—deforestation, for example. In Plato's dialogue *Critias*, the Athenian aristocrat after whom the dialogue is named draws a nostalgic contrast between present and past.

> What now remains compared with what existed then [he says], is like the skeleton of a sick man, all the fat and soft earth wasted away and only the bare framework of the land left. . . . The country was once unspoiled: its mountains were arable highlands and what is now stony fields was once good soil. And the earth was enriched by the annual rains

> which were not lost as now by flowing from the bare land into the sea . . . but deep soil received and stored the water . . . there were forests on the mountains; there are some which now have nothing but food for bees that had trees not so very long ago and the rafters from those that were chopped down to roof the large buildings are still sound.

And there are many features of Greek soil and climate that have never changed: the weather, for example. One has to live through a Greek summer to know why Pindar began his first Olympian ode with the bald statement, *Ariston men hudor,* "Water is best." I first read that line in England, where water is so plentiful that sometimes there doesn't seem to be anything else (someone once suggested that Thales, with his theory that all things are water, must have spent some time in England), and the line doesn't seem to make much sense. (Some schoolboy wit had, in fact, proposed a correction to the text in my book, *zythos* for *hudor,* to produce the meaning: "Beer is best.") It is only in Greece that one feels the true force of that magnificent opening phrase, when one has come, like the Greeks themselves, to prefer a glass of water in the heat to beer or lemonade or wine, to call, at the *kafeneion,* for more and more *neraiki;* only a Greek summer and the total dehydration two hours in the sun can produce will make one feel the full force of Pindar's words. But this is only one small example. One has to experience a Greek thunderstorm, with the lightning visible for miles and the thunder crash echoing from mountain to mountain through the clear air to feel the terror and majesty of the last scenes of the *Oedipus at Colonus,* to know what is meant by the thunderbolt Zeus brandishes with his right arm. And the sea does not change. Standing on the Acropolis looking down on the gulf at sunset, one can see what looks like wide tracks in the pattern of rough sea and smooth; they are surely Homer's "paths of the sea" (*hygra keleutha*). And one has to walk the bare Attic hills in the spring and see the incredible carpet of richly colored wild flowers springing from barren rock to understand why Pindar called Athens "violet crowned." With time, as the seasons change, as the olives are shaken from the trees, gathered and pressed, as the soil is plowed and sown, as much later the fruit begins to ripen and fall, as the grain is winnowed on the high circular threshing floor that must be the origin of the orchestra in which the tragic chorus danced, the scholar who has had the good fortune to spend a whole year in Greece can learn to feel the rhythm of the Greek seasons, of the Greek earth, a rhythm unlike that of his own country and one that has not changed since Hesiod wrote its rulebook and its praise.

So much for the land, but what of the people? The initial disappointment most Greek scholars feel when confronted for the first time by modern Greeks en masse is due solely to the illusions they bring with them. England and Germany were the two great centers of Greek studies in the nineteenth century, and both nations created a vision of the ancient Greeks that had more to do with their ideal of themselves than with reality. In this misconception they were encouraged by the fact that ancient Greek art was known to the nineteenth century mainly in the form of sculpture; Attic vases, which came mostly from Etruscan tombs, were labeled "Etruscan" vases until late in the century. And sculpture, at any rate the unpainted marble of the Parthenon frieze, allows the beholder to clothe its reticent surface in any colors he pleases. "If horses had gods they would look like horses," Xenophanes blandly observed long ago; and one has only to turn to the trashiest kind of English and American novels—the surest evidence of a people's deep-seated prejudices and most widely accepted clichés—to find what image of the ancient Greeks was formed in the Western mind. In such novels the hero is described, as often as not, as looking "like a Greek god." Investigation of the text generally reveals that he is a little over six feet tall and has blue eyes and pale golden hair. He looks, in fact, exactly like the Edwardian ideal of the Oxford undergraduate. No wonder the first sight of the crowds in Piraeus by day and Omonoia by night gives the Western classicist a jolt.

There is really no reason why it should. The vases with their black-haired and black-bearded figures and, still more, the painted archaic sculpture in the Acropolis museum give a picture of ancient Greeks who look startingly like the modern article. There is one *kore* in that museum, with black abundant hair and dark, wide eyes, whose modern sisters can be seen any day of the week walking down Hodos Stadiou. And in any case, the ancient literature gives no basis for this Western feeling (subliminal, but therefore all the stronger) that ancient Greeks were tall, blond, and blue-eyed. "Xanthos Menelaos" *may* have been blond, though the word more likely means red- or brown-haired, but surely the fact that he is so often called "xanthos" suggests that the other Achaian chieftains were not. And in Sophocles' *Antigone,* when the chorus wants to say "ever since I became an old man," they say "ever since my hair changed from *black* to white,"

. . . ἐξ ὅτου λευκὴν ἐγὼ
τήνδ' ἐκ μελαίνης ἀμφιβάλλομαι τρίχα

(ll. 1091 f.).

It is of course not only in his looks that the modern Greek resembles his ancestors. The men sitting in the *kafeneion* discussing the latest rumors and playing interminable games of *tavli* are no different from the men sitting by the fountain in Corinth playing *pessoi* (it seems to have been almost exactly the same game) from whom the *paedagogos* in Euripedes' *Medea* picked up the rumor that his mistress was to be banished. The ancient Greeks were famous racers, especially in chariots; anyone who is about to take his first taxi ride in central Athens would do well to prepare himself psychologically by reading the description of the chariot race in Sophocles' *Electra.* I once thought of writing a Pindaric ode in praise of a driver who got me through rush-hour traffic to the station mainly by driving on the sidewalks. To strike a more serious note, the same touchy sense of personal honor that is at the root of Achilles' wrath still governs relations between man and man in modern Greece; Greek society still fosters in the individual a fierce sense of his privileges, no matter how small, of his rights, no matter how confined, of his personal worth, no matter how low. And to defend it, he will stop, like Achilles, at nothing. Even its name is still the same, *filotimo, filotimia.* And of course on the larger scale of national politics, little has changed; modern Greek politics has no better analyst than Thucydides, whose somber description of Athens in the last decades of the fifth century B.C. reads like a foreshadowing of the tragic events of 1940–50. The more one lives in modern Greece, the more one is forced to see the modern in the light of the ancient and also to reread the ancient Greeks with new insights drawn from a knowledge of the modern.

And finally, the language. It is in some ways the most rewarding aspect of modern Greece for the classical scholar. A closer study of the spoken language reveals an intimate and live relationship between the languages of fifth- and twentieth-century Athens. Not only can the modern spoken language be called on to elucidate obscure words in ancient authors, as has been brilliantly done in some passages of Aristophanes, but also the scholar who learned his Greek as a dead language has in modern Greece the exhilarating experience of finding it alive: he can hear in the *laiki,* the open-air market, near Kolonaki every Friday the very tone of Aristophanes' sausage seller and market women and on the docks of Piraeus the sharp wit and banter of the sailors who manned the great fleets which set out from what is now Passalimani.

All the scholar has to do is to forget the artificial *katharevousa* of the newspaper editorials and government bureaucracy and listen to and learn from the popular speech of Greece, which is also, of course, the base from which the poets work. I ran up against the difficulties involved in the "language question" halfway through my year in Greece, which was 1960–61.

I had already been appointed director of Harvard's Center for Hellenic Studies in Washington but had not yet taken up its responsibilities. Professor Bakalakis of the University of Thessaloniki had somehow heard about the center and also tracked me down (I was keeping away from academic circles so that I could get some work done); he invited me to come to Thessaloniki to make a speech explaining what the center was. It was a good opportunity to try out my newly learned modern Greek and also perhaps to recruit some Greek fellows for the center (and in fact over the next twenty years no fewer than five young scholars came from Thessaloniki to spend a year at the center). I accepted and started to work on my speech.

On the overnight train going up to Saloniki I suddenly got cold feet. There I was, going to speak in the *dimotiki* I had learned talking to ordinary Athenians, to an academic audience on an academic subject. They might well think it, coming from a foreigner, presumptuous, even insulting. At the last stop before Thessaloniki, Larisa I think it was, I bought a whole clutch of newspapers and with the help of the editorials rewrote the speech in flowing *katharevousa.*

Next morning, at seven o'clock, we arrived. I had an appointment with Linos Politis at ten, so I walked around the town, especially along the magnificent seafront. My bag, however, was getting to be a nuisance; I happened to see the office of the American Express, went in and explained my situation, and asked if they could keep the bag for me, which, very courteously, they agreed to do.

Six or seven hours later, after a fascinating interview with Linos Politis, and a magnificent lunch in a restaurant on the waterfront, I was to be taken to my hotel for a rest before the speech and asked my host to stop by the American Express. To my horror, here was a big sign on the door ΚΛΕΙΣΤΟ. What's more, it wasn't going to open again until six—too late for me. The speech was due at five-thirty. So, once at the hotel, instead of a rest, I had to recompose the speech, in doublequick time, and this time there was no fooling around with the *katharevousa*.

The speech went off well. I had inserted two jokes to test the audience's comprehension of my imperfect accent—and they laughed at both places. Afterwards at dinner, I told Politis what had happened. For a moment I thought he look shocked and that I had made a mistake to tell him, but then he began to laugh. He laughed very loudly and went on laughing. And finally he said to me. "Your lucky *daimon* was at work. Leaving that second version at American Express was the best thing you could have done." And he proceeded to explain that Thessaloniki was, so to speak, the home and champion of *demotiki*, was writing its grammar and syntax—"If you had tried your warmed-up *katharevousa* on the audience, they would have tried hard not to laugh." I told him that I had been suddenly terrified by the memory of a professor of law at the University of Athens who had dominated an Athenian dinner party with long discussions in a very high flying *katharevousa*; he had been told I was a professor of ancient Greek and informed me that when he went to Munich the German professor there told him he spoke like Plato. "Oh," said Politis, in a tone of good-humored patience. "Athens..."

Even this distinction between an official quasi-literary language and popular speech goes back to antiquity; we still have handbooks written in the Roman imperial period that specify lists of acceptable "Attic" words and rule out others. And we know, from the private letters that have emerged, written on papyrus, from the sands of Egypt, that

Greeks there in the second century were speaking a Greek that had sometimes startling resemblances to the modern language. A boy's letter to his father, for example, in which the child asks to be taken along on a trip to Alexandria, begins, exactly as a modern schoolboy might begin: *Lipon, pater mou* . . . "Well, father . . ." Not only is the word *loipon* (as it was spelled in fifth-century Athens and still is) used in its modern sense of "well"; the boy's phonetic spelling shows that the itacism which is such a pronounced feature of the modern language had already begun.

"It is strange," says George Thomson in his brilliant book, *The Greek Language,* "that so many scholars visiting Greece to refresh themselves at the fount of Hellenism should spend all their time contemplating the material remains of antiquity without realizing that the object of their quest still flows from the lips of the people." In this aspect of modern Greece are great treasures of new insight and fresh understanding ready for the classical scholar to discover, and without the pains of excavation. All he has to do is learn and listen. And also read, for the great poets of modern Greece—and Western Europe is slowly realizing that they are among the world's greatest poets, Cavafy, Seferis, Sikelianos, Elytis, Kazantzakis—all of them are heirs to the legacy of ancient Greece, which is both a blessing and a burden; all of them draw strength from the tradition even as they try to maintain their independence of it.

What modern Greece offers the student of classical literature and thought is just as great as what it offers the archaeologist, if not greater. It can renew and refresh his contact with the ancient sources in hundreds of ways. Above all, he can ground in Greek earth that *Nephelokykyggia,* the "ideal" Greece he has conjured up from books; it will enable him at last "to give to airy nothing a local habitation and a name."

LECTURERS

Provost's Lecture Series   1985–88

Since 1985, the following speakers have appeared in the Provost's Lecture Series:

Mrs. Virginia B. Ball—Member of the Board, Ball State University Foundation

Dr. Glen W. Bowersock—Professor of Ancient History, The Institute for Advanced Study, Princeton University

The Honorable Dr. John Brademas—President, New York University; Former Member of Congress

Dr. Richard Burkhardt—Professor Emeritus of History, Former Provost and Vice President for Academic Affairs, Ball State University

Mrs. Dorothy Burkhardt—Former Instructor of Foreign Languages, Ball State University

Dr. Richard J. Cebula—Professor of Economics, Emory University

Dr. John E. Corbally—President, John D. and Catherine T. MacArthur Foundation, Chicago

Sir James Craig, G.O.M.G.—British Ambassador to Syria (1976–79) and to Saudi Arabia (1979–84); Director General, The Middle East Association

Mrs. Nancy Crawshaw—Royal Institute for International Affairs, Adviser to the House of Commons Foreign Affairs Select Committee, and Journalist

Dr. John Demos—Professor of American History, Yale University

Dr. E. Inman Fox—Professor of Hispanic Studies, Northwestern University

The Right Honorable Lord Grenfell—The World Bank, Washington, D.C.

Dr. Arthur J. R. Groom—Professor of International Relations, Rutherford College, University of Kent at Canterbury

The Honorable Lee H. Hamilton—Member, United States House of Representatives (D.-Ind.); Chairman, Subcommittee on Europe and the Middle East, House Foreign Affairs Committee; Chairman, Permanent Select Committee on Intelligence; Chairman, Joint Economic Committee

Dr. George H. Hanford—President, The College Board

Mr. Paul Henze—Staff Member, National Security Council (1977–80); Fellow, Woodrow Wilson International Center for Scholars (1980–81); Foreign Area Adviser, Rand Corporation

Dr. Hans Heymann, Jr.—Senior Research Fellow, The Hudson Institute

Dr. Barbara Jelavich—Professor of History, Indiana University

Sir Curtis Keeble, G.O.M.G.—Diplomat, United Kingdom; Former Ambassador to the U.S.S.R.

Dr. Bernard M. W. Knox—Professor Emeritus of Classics, Harvard University; Director Emeritus, Center for Hellenic Studies, Washington, D.C.

Miss Ellen Laipson—Congressional Research Service/Foreign, The Library of Congress

Dr. Myron Lieberman, Professor, Ohio University

Dr. Arthur S. Link—Professor of American History, Princeton University

Dr. Leslie Lipson—Professor of Political Science, University of California, Berkeley

Sir Donald Maitland—Diplomat, United Kingdom

Dr. Fergus Millar—Camden Professor of Ancient History and Fellow, Brasenose College, Oxford

Dr. Charles C. Moskos—Professor of Sociology, Northwestern University

Miss Daphne Park, C.M.G., O.B.E.—Diplomat; Principal, Somerville College; Pro-Vice Chancellor, Oxford University

The Honorable Sir Peter Ramsbotham, G.C.M.G., G.C.V.O.—British Ambassador to Iran (1974–74); Ambassador to the United States (1974–77); Governor of Bermuda (1977–78); Director of Lloyds Bank and of Commercial Union Assurance Company

The Honorable William Ruckelshaus—Former Administrator, Environmental Protection Agency

The Honorable Paul S. Sarbanes—Member, United States Senate (D.-Md.); Chairman, Joint Economic Committee; Member, Foreign Relations Committee; Chairman, Senate Subcommittee on Middle East

The Honorable Phil Sharp—Member, United States House of Representatives (D.-Ind.); Chairman, Subcommittee on Energy and Power, House Energy and Commerce Committee; Member, Interior and Insular Affairs Committee

Mr. Charles Silberman—Director, Study of Jewish Life

Ms. Janet W. Solinger—Director, Resident Associate Program, The Smithsonian Institution

Dr. Robert W. Thomson—Director, Dumbarton Oaks, Washington, D.C.

Dr. Karl J. Weintraub—Thomas E. Donnelley Distinguished Service Professor, The University of Chicago

Dr. F. J. West, Jr.—Vice President, The Hudson Institute

Dr. Bryan R. Wilson—Senior Fellow and Professor of Sociology, All Souls College, Oxford

Mr. Brian Winston—Dean, School of Communications, The Pennsylvania State University